DIGITAL QUICK GUIDE™

S0-BZE-825

DIGITAL
PHOTOGRAPHY 101

LEARN HOW EASY IT IS TO CREATE
DAZZLING DIGITAL IMAGES!

Michelle Perkins

AMHERST MEDIA, INC. ■ BUFFALO, NY

Published by:
Amherst Media, Inc.
P.O. Box 586
Buffalo, N.Y. 14226
Fax: 716-874-4508
www.AmherstMedia.com

Publisher: Craig Alesse
Assistant Editor: Barbara A. Lynch-Johnt

ISBN: 1-58428-160-X
Library of Congress Card Catalog Number: 2004113076

Printed in Korea.
10 9 8 7 6 5 4 3 2 1

TABLE OF CONTENTS

INTRODUCTION

As photographers, of whatever skill levels and special interests, we have the distinct pleasure of being involved in photography at a time when the art form is undergoing its biggest changes in decades. Not since the advent of color photography has there been such a revolution in the field!

This book is for anyone who wants to get started using these new technologies and learn how to make the most of digital imaging. Whether you are shopping for your first digital camera or have been using digital for a while but feel you need a stronger grasp of the concepts to maximize your results, you'll find information here that will fit the bill.

Digital imaging has made it possible to take total control of your photos and create images that were previously either very time consuming or flat-out impossible. You can shoot hundreds of frames without having to pay a cent for film or developing—and sharing each dazzling new creation with your whole family is as easy as sending out an e-mail.

The digital revolution has, for a lot of people, put the fun back in photography. By increasing control and reducing disappointing surprises (Mom's eyes were closed!), digital has made it easier for everyone to create memorable images. With the techniques in this book, you'll be well on your way to mastering this powerful technology and taking better digital pictures!

1. GETTING STARTED

As with anything else, however, the new privileges of digital also come with new responsibilities. The following are some of the issues to consider.

■ NEW CHALLENGES

With film, if a print came out looking terrible, your lab probably reprinted it at no charge (unless the negative was really badly exposed; then you were just plain out of luck). With digital, *you* are responsible for making sure that your images look just right. Whether you print them on an inkjet printer or take them to a lab, how you handle the files will determine how good your prints will look. If digital prints come out poorly, it's usually because the image file isn't right (it could be too dark, too low in contrast, have a color cast, etc.).

Digital gives you instant results. You know right away that you did or did not get the shot.

With digital, you'll probably also find that you shoot a lot more pictures—maybe several times more than you would have on film. Once you get home, though, you're going to somehow need to archive all of these images so you can find them later. That can be time consuming.

Oh—and what happens when you (or a less technically savvy friend) accidentally delete a folder full of photos from your hard drive? Ouch. But relax . . . the news is definitely not all bad!

■ NEW ADVANTAGES

The good news is that once you figure out how to adjust your photos so they print well, you should get great results with virtually every print. I don't know about you, but that's something I never quite got from my film lab. (If your film lab was great, though, see if they can print your digital files so you can continue to enjoy their expertise!)

On a related note, there's another *huge* advantage to digital: retouching. With film, it wasn't financially feasible for most people to have their everyday images retouched. With digital, there's no reason you have to live with blemishes, ex-boyfriends, or other annoying distractions in your images.

Yes, there will be challenges when archiving your images (we'll deal with that on pages 82–83). What's more important, though, is that more images mean more chances to get great shots—and you can always delete the images that don't work out!

Last but not least, digital photography gives you instant results. You know right away whether you did or did not get the shot. If you did, you can relax; if you didn't, you can reshoot before the subject walks away.

In the end, most people find that the instant results and increased control of making the change to digital are well worth their while—and with a little knowledge, that even the challenges are quite manageable.

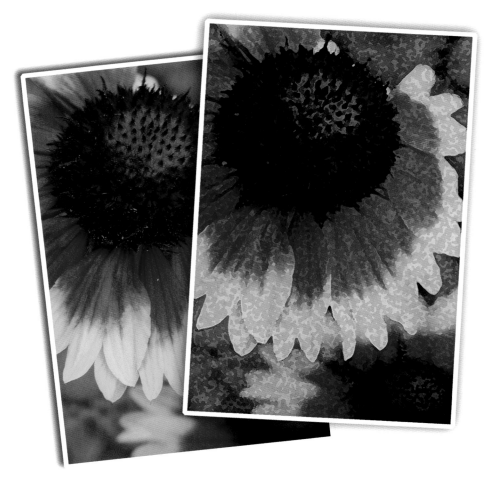

With digital-imaging software, it only takes a few seconds to add interesting effects to your images.

2. RESOLUTION, PART 1

Digital images are made up of dots called pixels. The resolution of an image tells us how close together those dots are (the dots per inch—referred to as the "dpi" of an image). Images with dots that are close together are said to have a "high" resolution (a high number of dots per inch). Images with dots that are far apart are said to have a "low" resolution.

■ A (MOSTLY) FIXED TOTAL

The total number of pixels in an image is, for the most part, a fixed value. (See pages 11–12 for how to change the number of dots in an image when needed.) You can think of the data in an image as being like a cup full of coffee. When the coffee is in the cup, it has a small surface area, but it's pretty deep. If you poured the coffee out on the floor, the exact same amount would cover a lot more area, but it would also be much shallower. (Note: It's really better to just drink your coffee, but if you must try this experiment for yourself, be sure to have plenty of paper towels on hand.)

With a digital file that has, let's say, 4000 total pixels, the same principle applies. If you used those pixels to create an image that was only 1"x1", the pixels would be quite close together (the equivalent of the full cup of coffee). If you made an image that was 12"x12", that limited number of pixels would have to spread out quite a bit in order to cover the larger area. As a result, the resolution would be quite a bit lower (the equivalent of the spilled cup of coffee).

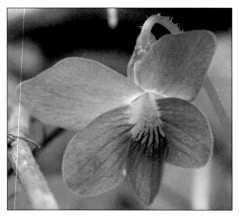 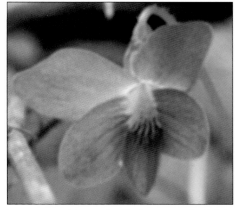

The resolution your image needs to be depends on how you want to use it. The image on the left is at 300dpi, perfect for printing in a book. The image on the right is at 72dpi. This would look just fine on a web site, but its resolution is too low to look good in print.

A GRAY AREA

Which is bigger, the image on the left or the one on the right? Actually, it all depends on how you look at it. The image on the right definitely covers more space, but both 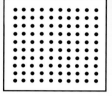 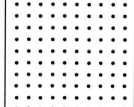 images are made up of the same number of identical dots. In the image on the left, the dots are tightly packed, giving it a high resolution (a high number of dots per inch). In the image on the right, the dots are far apart, giving it a low resolution (low number of dots per inch).

■ SO WHY SHOULD I CARE?

The resolution of an image, to a great degree, determines the apparent quality of the image. High-resolution images tend to look clear and sharp—more like photographs. Low-resolution images tend to look somewhat grainy, speckled, and blurry.

Does this mean you should always use the highest resolution possible? Well, no. The more dots in an image, the more the computer has to remember and move around every time you ask it to do something with those dots. This means it will take longer for the image to open, and performing operations on it will be slower. It will also take longer to upload or download online.

When digital cameras are advertised, you'll notice that one of the first specifications listed for each model is the size of the file it is capable of creating. This is usually listed in megapixels (see pages 18–19). The larger the file, the more possibilities you'll have for your images—that's why more is usually better in a digital camera. More pixels mean you can make bigger prints or crop the image more dramatically to improve the composition (see pages 62–63).

3. RESOLUTION, PART 2

So, what should the resolution of your image be? The answer is: only as high as it has to be. The precise number of pixels will be determined by how you will use the image.

■ WHICH RESOLUTION IS RIGHT?

If you want to use an image on your web page, you'll select a relatively low resolution—probably 72dpi. This is all that is needed to create an acceptably sharp image on a monitor. Anything more wouldn't make the image look any better and would increase the time the image takes to load (and, remember, the majority of Internet users still rely on slower dial-up connections!).

If you want to generate a photo-quality print on your inkjet printer, you may want to create a file as large as 700dpi. Check the manual that came with your printer to determine the resolutions recommended for its various print settings.

If you'll be having someone else (like a photo lab) print your image, ask them what they recommend. For more on this, see pages 76–77.

■ CHANGING RESOLUTION

Most digital-imaging software allows you to change the resolution of an image. As nice as this sounds, though, it really doesn't take the place of proper planning.

Most software does a good job of moving around existing dots (making them closer together or farther apart), and many applications are even pretty skilled at removing dots (reducing resolution). What they don't do very well is allow you to turn 50 dots into 500 dots. If you ask your software to do this, the program will have to guess where to put these dots and what they should look like. Invariably, it won't guess 100 percent successfully, and your resulting image will appear blurry.

Sooner or later, this is going to cause you a big headache—you'll desperately want to make a huge poster and just not have the dots you need. Trust me—every digital imager has been there. It's such a common problem, in fact, that software has been designed specifically to cope with it. Genuine Fractals (www.lizardtech.com), pxl SmartScale (www.extensis.com), PhotoZoom and PhotoZoom Pro (www.trulyphotomagic.com), and plug-ins (see pages 60–61) like SI Pro (www.fredmiranda.com) all provide high-quality upscaling.

A word to the wise: before investing your hard-earned cash, make sure that the software you are interested in works with your digital-imaging program and operating system!

■ DON'T JUST GUESS

If you're not sure what resolution you need in your image in order to create the product you have in mind, find out *before* you create your file. There's no point in wasting your time to make complicated refinements on an image that turns out to be unusable.

If you'll be using your image in multiple applications (say you want to make a print but also plan to e-mail the photo to someone), create your image at the largest size you'll need. Make any needed corrections to this large file, then reduce its size and save multiple copies of the image for other uses.

IT'S *HOW* BIG?

There are two things to keep in mind when creating a digital image. First, ask yourself what the final dimensions of the image need to be. Do you want to make a billboard or a postage stamp? Next, determine what the final resolution of the image needs to be—72dpi? 300dpi? 1000dpi? Once you know the answers to these questions, you'll be ready to create an image (or determine if an existing image will suit your needs). All you need to do is multiply the resolution by the dimensions of the image. Here's how:

Imagine you're making a photo to put in a newsletter. The image needs to be 2" tall and 3" wide on the page, and your printer has told you that the resolution should be 300dpi. To make a file the right size, multiply 2" x 300dpi (for the height) and 3" x 300dpi (for the width). This tells you that you need an image that is 600 pixels tall and 900 pixels wide (600x900).

Later, one of the people in the photo asks if she can have a copy of this file to make an 8"x10" photo-quality print on her inkjet printer. She needs a final resolution of 700dpi. Will the same file work? Nope—your friend will need a much larger image file, one that is 5600 pixels wide (8" x 700dpi) and 7000 pixels tall (10" x 700dpi).

---

4. DIGITAL COLOR

Each pixel in an image is assigned a color. It's the combination of these differently colored pixels that creates the picture we see when we look at an image. Knowing how these colors are created can be quite helpful.

■ PRIMARY COLORS

If you ever took an art class (or played with watercolors as a kid), you probably know that combining two or more colors creates new colors. For example,

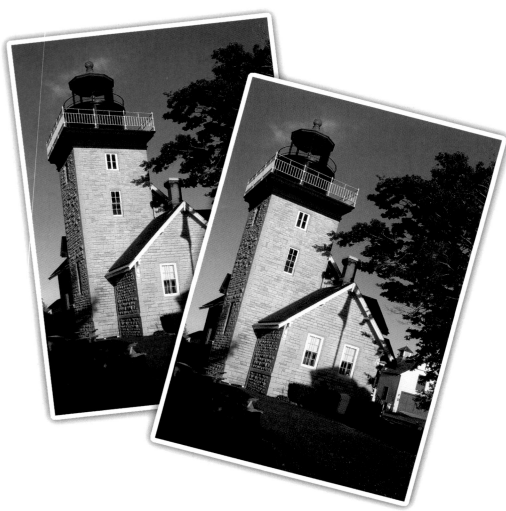

To instantly convert a color image to a black & white one, you can simply change the image to the Grayscale mode.

combining blue and yellow paint makes green paint. In fact, almost all colors are actually combinations of some other colors. The exceptions (the very few colors you can't create by combining others) are called primary colors. The primary colors are divided into two sets: additive and subtractive.

■ COLOR MODES

In digital imaging, the set of primary colors that are used to create all the other colors in your image is collectively referred to as the color mode.

RGB Mode. If you combine varying amounts of R (red), G (green), and B (blue), you can create about 16.7 million other colors. Because of this, RGB is described as having a wide gamut, a term used to describe the total range of colors that can be produced. As you'll quickly learn when you begin working with digital images, however, the RGB gamut, wide as it may be, is still not as wide as the gamut perceived by the human eye. As a result, subtle colors that your eyes can distinguish in a scene may render as a single tone in RGB. This doesn't normally present a tremendous problem, but it's a deficiency in color range that we just have to learn to live with.

> Subtle colors that your eyes can distinguish in a scene may render as a single tone in RGB.

Grayscale Mode. The Grayscale color mode consists of only one channel—black. In this mode, the pixels are assigned values from 0 (white) to 100 (black). Everything in between these two values will be a shade of gray. Because this mode only has black, white, and gray tones, you can turn a color image into a black & white one by using your image-editing software to change to the Grayscale mode.

CMYK Mode. This color mode consists of four channels: cyan, magenta, yellow, and black. It is the color mode used for process-color printing—the type of printing that is used to create magazines, books, posters, and other items. If you need to prepare an image to be printed in a magazine or book, you'll need to convert it to CMYK before sending it to the printer.

5. IMAGE FILE FORMATS

Think of the file format as the language in which the digital image is written. It tells applications, like word processing software or web browsers, that your file is a picture (rather than a text file, for example) and how it should handle all the data in the file to display it correctly on the screen. The file format is indicated by a tag (.TIF .JPG, etc.) added after the file name.

■ COMPATIBILITY

If you travel to France and try to speak Portuguese to the natives, you'll likely encounter some comprehension problems. The same thing can happen when you ask a program to understand a digital file that doesn't speak its language. Some programs are multilingual; they "speak" a wide variety of file formats. Other programs recognize only one or two file formats. If you plan to use your digital image in several programs, read the software's manual to determine what formats it accepts, then save your image accordingly.

■ COMPRESSION

Some file formats give you the option of reducing the amount of memory your computer will need to store an image. This is called compression. By reducing the memory required to store an image (i.e., the file size), compression allows more images to be stored in a smaller space and permits them to be transmitted over the Internet more quickly.

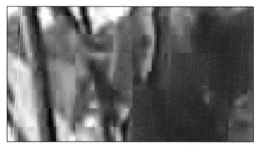
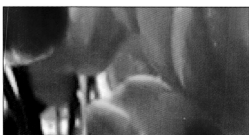

If this sounds too good to be true, don't worry—it is (at least to some degree). Imagine you crush a soda can. It will take up less space, but it will never look like it did to begin with. With digital compression, the same principle applies—of course, it's more sophisticated, and your images won't look as bad as your soda can.

When an image is enlarged, you can really start to see the difference in quality between JPEG compression (top) and LZW (bottom).

14

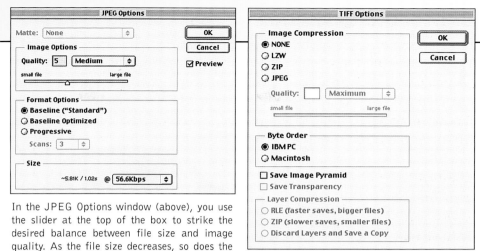

In the JPEG Options window (above), you use the slider at the top of the box to strike the desired balance between file size and image quality. As the file size decreases, so does the image quality. In the TIFF Options window (right) from Adobe Photoshop Elements, you can choose to save your file with no compression, LZW, ZIP, or JPEG compression.

When an image is compressed, equations are applied to arrange the data more efficiently or to remove data that is deemed to be extraneous. As a result, your image won't look as good. However, the quality may not be objectionable—or it may be worth it to have an image that loads quickly. Two file formats that offer compression are JPEG and TIFF.

JPEG offers "lossy" compression, meaning that it removes data and degrades the image to some degree. You can, however, control the degree of compression, so you can compress the file just a little (for better image quality) or a whole lot (when quality isn't as important). The characteristic grid pattern created by JPEG compression (see facing page) becomes especially apparent when an image is saved and resaved, compressing it each time. For works in progress, this is not a good file format, but it's standard on the Internet because of the small file sizes it produces.

TIFF offers "lossless" compression called LZW, which doesn't throw any data out (so the image quality remains better), but it also can't compress the image as much. The new JPEG 2000 format also allows you to use "lossless" compression.

You can also select ZIP compression from the TIFF Options window. This is similar to LZW, but it adds a layer of protection that helps reduce the likelihood of corruption when files are sent across the Internet.

15

6. DIGITAL CAMERAS: TYPES

There are several types of digital cameras. You can use any type—and you don't need to use the latest model—but some types and models of cameras do offer features that make them more flexible than others. Additionally, it's important to make sure that the camera you choose is comfortable for you to work with—if you have large hands and a tiny camera with tiny buttons, you may find it quite frustrating.

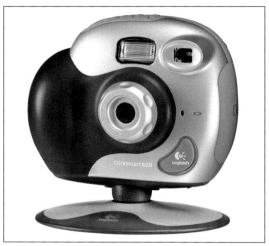

Webcams fall into the minicam class.

■ MINICAMS

Minicams, little digital cameras that shoot (usually) low resolution images, are now found in everything from cellular phones to PDAs. In the same class as these are webcams, which can take quick shots and video clips for online use. Some very low-end digital cameras (which take screen-resolution [640x480-pixel] images) also fall into this category. These are lots of fun (and great for images you'll only use online), but their low resolution limits your options when it comes to making prints.

■ POINT-AND-SHOOTS

The most common type of digital camera is the point-and-shoot—the kind of camera that most nonprofessionals choose. This type of camera has a built-in lens, fully automatic exposure and focusing, and an image sensor (the "film" of the digital camera) in the 2–6 megapixel range.

It is helpful to use a model with a zoom lens, since this will give you the most choices when composing your images. Also helpful is a full range of exposure settings (like a landscape mode, aperture/shutter priority, etc.—we'll be discussing these in more detail on pages 42–43). Being able to select your aperture and shutter speed manually are also helpful, as is the option to focus manually (although this can be so tricky to adjust on point-and-shoots that you may find it too frustrating to use).

Look for a model that gives you several white-balance settings (including the option to create a custom setting, which will be discussed in greater detail on pages 22–23).

All of the major camera manufacturers—Kodak, Sony, Fuji, Nikon, Canon, etc.—make excellent cameras, so shop by feature rather than by brand name if you decide to purchase a new camera.

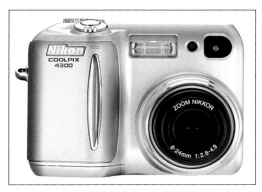

A point-and-shoot digital camera can produce excellent images.

■ DIGITAL SLRS

Digital SLR (single-lens-reflex) cameras are the most common type used by professional photographers. Because manufacturers have seen a rise in consumer interest in this type of camera (and because prices on digital cameras in general have continued to drop), some of these models are now priced under $1000—making them a real option for more

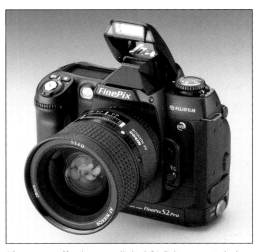

If you can afford one, a digital SLR is a great choice.

photographers. There are two types: those with interchangeable lenses and those without. The ability to change lenses is a great asset, giving you the ultimate flexibility when creating your images—but these models are also higher in cost. Digital SLRs usually have an image sensor in the 6- to 10-megapixel range (this number is increasing rapidly). They also offer more advanced metering and focusing features than point-and-shoot models and more flexible flash settings. Digital SLRs also offer manual focusing, aperture, and shutter control—letting you take control of your images much more easily than with a point-and-shoot model.

7. DIGITAL CAMERAS: MEGAPIXELS

Resolution has been an important issue with digital cameras from the beginning. The more pixels you have in your image, the larger the prints you can make, the more fine detail you'll be able to capture, the more you can crop and still be left with a usable number of pixels, etc. More pixels, however, almost always means a higher ticket price.

■ WHAT'S A MEGAPIXEL?

When you look at an ad for digital cameras or peruse a display of them at your local electronics superstore, the one specification you can be sure you'll see listed for every model is the size of the images its sensor can capture. This will be listed in one of two ways.

First, it may be listed as the pixel dimensions—like "1280x960 pixels," meaning that the image sensor captures an image that is 1280 pixels wide and 960 pixels tall (think of it like measuring the dimensions of a room). Second, the size of the image sensor may be listed in terms of megapixels. The number of megapixels a camera's sensor can produce is determined by multiplying the width of the sensor (in pixels) by the height and dividing by one million. For example:

$$1280 \times 960 = 1{,}228{,}800$$
$$1{,}228{,}800 \div 1{,}000{,}000 = 1.2288$$

This tells us that a camera with a sensor that records 1280x960 pixels could also be said to record 1.2288 megapixels (this will normally be rounded up, so the camera will be listed as a 1.3-megapixel model).

PRINT SIZE VS. MEGAPIXELS

The following are approximate minimum megapixel requirements for creating a variety of print sizes. These calculations assume that the print is being made at 200dpi. Some print processes may require lower or higher resolutions.

PRINT SIZE	MIN. MEGAPIXELS
4"x6"	.6 megapixel
5"x7"	1.3 megapixels
8"x10"	3.2 megapixels
11"x14"	6.1 megapixels
16"x20"	11 megapixels

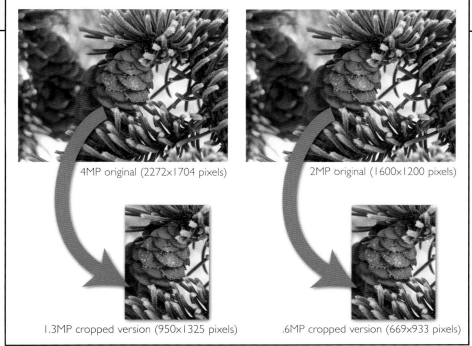

4MP original (2272x1704 pixels)

2MP original (1600x1200 pixels)

1.3MP cropped version (950x1325 pixels)

.6MP cropped version (669x933 pixels)

When significant cropping is needed, it helps to have a larger original file. Here, having a 4-megapixel original (left) gives us the flexibility to crop out most of the original image and still have enough data left to make a 5"x7" print. Starting with only a 2-megapixel file (right), making the same crop would leave only enough data for a 3"x4" print.

■ HOW MANY DO I NEED?

Most consumer digital cameras now feature a sensor of sufficient size (usually in the 3-megapixel neighborhood) to create nice 8"x10" prints—the largest size most people regularly make. Even low-end models usually have at least a 1.3-megapixel sensor, fine for making 5"x7" prints. Bottom-of-the-line cameras may capture only a .3-megapixel image (640x480 pixels).

What should you get? First, you'll need to decide on the largest size print you are likely to want to make. Don't skimp—if you think you *might* want to make some 8"x10" prints, don't settle for a 1.3-megapixel camera. If, on the other hand, all you want to do is post pictures of your items for sale on eBay, there's not much point in shelling out for a 6.1-megapixel model.

You might decide you like digital so much that you buy a larger model, say a 4-megapixel point-and-shoot, for family pictures and special events, as well as a cheap little 1.3-megapixel model to keep in your backpack or pop in your pocket for spur-of-the-moment snapshots—like when you run into Elvis ordering a latte for Marilyn Monroe at the corner coffee shop.

8. DIGITAL CAMERAS: IMAGE-SENSOR CHIPS

Image-sensor chips are the digital equivalent of film. Instead of light-sensitive materials that must be processed in chemicals in order to make the images appear, image-sensor chips use millions of tiny photo sensors to record the light that makes up an image. When light strikes one of these sensors, information about the quantity and color of the light is recorded. The readings are then processed electronically in order to turn this raw data into part of an image. When the data from all of the millions of individual sensors is combined, the result is a complete digital image.

Image sensors come in many sizes. How many light-sensing diodes a sensor has will determine how much data it can record. With most sensors, each individual diode is equivalent to one pixel in the image.

■ TYPES OF SENSORS

There are two types of image-sensor chips: CCD (charge-coupled device) and CMOS (complementary metal oxide semiconductor). Both are made of sili-

DIGITAL NOISE

Noise is the digital equivalent of film grain—tiny irregularities that manifest as specks and spots. Noise is usually thought of as a bad thing because it represents an "error" in the recording of an image. However, noise can also be a good thing—it can prevent digital images from looking too artificially smooth, it can sometimes be added to an image to disguise other problems (like distortions caused by JPEG compression), and it can even be created 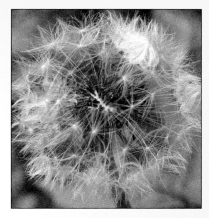 intentionally to add a mysterious or gritty look to an image. In digital, as with film, higher ISOs (the measurement of the degree of light sensitivity in a image-sensor chip or film) mean more noise; lower settings produce images with less noise. Noise can also be the result of disturbances in the currents generated by CCD or CMOS image sensors—disturbances that can be caused, for example, by electronic interference, heat, mechanical instability, etc.

con and both have millions of tiny light sensors. The main difference between the two types of chips has to do with how they handle data once it is collected by the individual sensors. With a CCD chip, this data is moved from the chip to other on-board electronics to be converted into usable digital values. With a CMOS chip, the conversion takes place within the individual light-sensitive element of the chip.

■ DOES IT MATTER?

So what does all this mean for digital-camera users? Well, for a

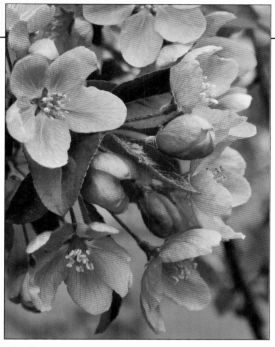

The Canon Digital Rebel, the camera this image was taken with, incorporates a CMOS image-sensor chip. Photograph by Roger W. Perkins.

long time, CCD chips were the image sensors of choice for digital cameras— and they are still by far the most common chip used in consumer models. CCDs provide excellent image quality and produce relatively little noise (see facing page). However, because these chips require a separate processor to handle the data recorded by the individual sensors, they require special manufacturing processes that make them rather pricey to produce. Cameras designed around CCD image sensors actually require several chips (as many as eight) to record and process image data.

Because the data processing in a CMOS chip occurs right on the image sensor itself, it's possible to design cameras that can actually function with only one chip. As you can image, that means much lower production costs. It also helps to reduce the required size of the camera and to minimize battery consumption—both good things for most digital-camera users. CMOS image-sensor chips are now being used in many large-format professional cameras, digital SLRs, and even some consumer cameras. Canon, in particular, has aggressively begun using CMOS chips in their new digital SLRs—including the Digital Rebel, one of the most affordable digital SLRs on the market.

9. DIGITAL CAMERAS: FEATURES

Digital cameras are, on the whole, a lot more sophisticated than film cameras. When buying a digital camera (or learning to use a model you already have), here are some things to look for.

■ IMAGE MODES

Most cameras offer several preset shooting options—generally designed to produce good results with a particular kind of subject. These often include a sports mode, a landscape mode, a portrait mode, etc. These modes will be covered in detail on pages 42–43.

■ WHITE-BALANCE SETTINGS

Color accuracy is important; we want our reds to look red, our greens to look green, and our skin tones to look natural and healthy. Digital cameras are equipped with white-balance settings that allow the camera to compensate and balance the colors for accuracy under just about any kind of light—sunlight, fluorescent light, tungsten light, etc.

Most cameras also offer auto white-balance settings, where the camera evaluates each individual shot and tries to create an ideal color balance for the scene. This is great for snapshots, especially when you are moving quickly and don't want to reset the white balance for each type of lighting you encounter.

The custom white-balance setting is great when you want to take a bunch of pictures under the same lighting conditions and make sure they all match. Imagine you wanted to take a series of portraits of the people at a family reunion. You could set up a custom white-balance setting for the area where you wanted to take the pictures (say, the

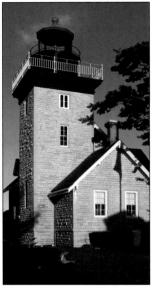

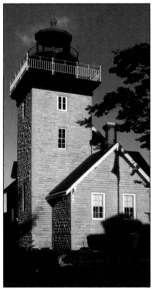

The top image was shot with the white balance set to auto. The bottom image was shot with the daylight setting. As you can see, the color rendition is quite different—although both are certainly acceptable.

BATTERIES

Digital cameras can really chew through batteries! Battery life will depend on a lot of variables—the camera model, the battery type, how often you shoot with flash, how long you leave the LCD screen on, etc. Keep in mind that most cameras employ proprietary battery packs, so getting back to shooting when your battery dies isn't just a matter of grabbing a new one at the corner drugstore—it could take a few hours to recharge a dead battery. Therefore, if it's in your budget, having a backup battery on hand isn't a bad idea. On the road, consider purchasing an adapter that lets you charge your battery from the car's cigarette lighter—much better than having to wait until you get home or back to your hotel to recharge!

backyard) and then photograph each subject. When it came time to frame a group of photos, you'd be sure that the colors would all match (the grass would not be a little more yellow in one image and a little more blue in another, etc.).

■ AUTO VS. MANUAL
Speaking of auto and manual settings, depending on the camera, you may also find the option to make your exposures manually, rather than automatically. If you are familiar with f-stops and shutter speeds, you may want to try this.

■ PANORAMICS
Many cameras now offer a mode that helps you shoot a sequence of images that you can later use software to combine into a single panoramic shot, a long, narrow photograph that often shows as much as a 360-degree view of a scene. For more on this, see page 58.

■ DIGITAL VIDEO CLIPS
Most point-and-shoot cameras let you produce short, low-resolution movies. They can also, however, eat up lots of space on your memory card, so be sure to buy a large media card if you think you'll want to shoot these.

10. DIGITAL CAMERAS: MEMORY CARDS

Memory cards come in all shapes, colors, and sizes—and you can now pick them up at drugstores, photo labs, and just about anywhere else you used to purchase film.

■ WHAT THEY ARE

Although they are sometimes referred to as the digital equivalent of film,

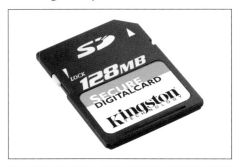

memory cards don't actually have anything to do with capturing an image—that's the job of the image sensor. Once the image sensor has captured the photo, it transfers the data to the memory card where it is stored. Unlike film, memory cards can also be used again and again.

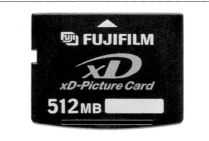

■ TYPES

There are two basic types of cards: flash memory and microdrives.

Flash memory cards are solid state, meaning there are no moving parts; electronics rather than mechanics do the work in these cards. There are many card formats within this group. The CompactFlash (CF) type is probably the most common, but Memory Stick, Secure Digital (SD), xD, and SmartMedia are also popular. These cards have several advantages: they are lightweight, noiseless, reliable, and save images quickly. The main disadvantage is their cost, which can be quite high.

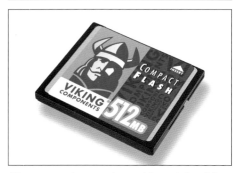

Memory cards come in a wide variety of formats and capacities from a number of different manufacturers. Before buying a digital camera, you might want to research the cost of the memory cards it requires—some formats cost a bit more than others!

Microdrives, on the other hand, are miniature hard drives (just like in your computer). Because microdrives feature internal moving parts, they are more delicate than flash cards. While flash memory cards can survive some serious abuse, even dropping a microdrive can cause problems.

Why doesn't everybody just use flash memory? Microdrives are much cheaper and the capacity of each card is much higher. This is especially important with cameras like digital SLRs that create very large files—meaning you will need lots of storage space in order to shoot numerous images without having to change cards.

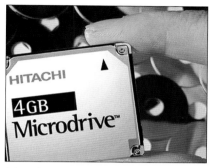

■ CAPACITY

Memory cards are labeled (and priced) according to their storage capacity. The

Microdrives are more delicate than flash memory cards, but they offer much higher storage capacities at more reasonable prices.

smallest ones hold only 8MB of data, while the largest now hold over 4G. The size of your camera's image sensor, the file format you choose to shoot, and the amount of compression you set your camera to use (sometimes called the image-quality setting) will determine how many images a particular memory card will hold.

With digital, people tend to shoot a lot more images than they did on film, so don't skimp—with a large card, you can shoot for hours and never have to swap it out (so you'll never miss a shot). For most people, a 256MB card is really the smallest comfortable option for a day of shooting (say, on a vacation)—and a 512MB card is very nice. Still, it's always a good idea to have a backup card with you, just in case.

FORMATTING THE CARD

After you've transferred all the images off a card and backed them up (at least once) to CD-R or DVD-R, return the card to your camera and select the "format" option from your in-camera menu (consult your camera's manual for more information on this) to remove all the images. Formatting the card, rather than just deleting all the images, completely resets the card and helps prevent potential problems and disc errors.

11. DIGITAL CAMERAS: LCDs, VIEWFINDERS

Probably the most noticeable difference between film cameras and digital cameras is the LCD screen on the back of the digitals. This has really changed the way we take pictures. For one thing, you don't need to hold the camera up to your eye anymore; you can hold it at arm's length, over your head, etc.

■ LCD SCREEN

The LCD screen on the back of a digital camera is, by and large, your means of interacting with the camera. There are a few buttons and dials, but a lot of your settings will be made using the on-screen menus. Of course, most people also compose their images using this screen and use it to review the images they have already shot. That makes the LCD screen a very important feature. So what should you look for?

First, think about the size of the screen. Larger screens mean bigger image previews—and for most people, that means an easier experience composing and reviewing images. After all, it's pretty tough to get a good idea of what your image looks like when it's the size of a postage stamp! With cameras getting smaller and smaller, though, many LCD screens are also shrinking. That may be okay for a camera you just want to have in your bag for everyday snapshots of friends and family, but it may not be the best option for a camera you want to use to take breathtaking landscape images on your once-in-a-lifetime trip to China. Larger screens are also good for people whose eyes are maybe not what they used to be—so if you have any vision concerns, go for a model with a larger screen.

Also important is the legibility of the menus on the screen. Check that the type is large enough and bright enough to read easily. You have enough things to worry about when crafting your images without having to struggle to read the menu options.

STRETCH THE JUICE

The LCD screen is a big battery drain. Therefore, most cameras let you turn off the LCD screen when it's not in use—without turning off the camera. Digitals usually take a few seconds to boot up when you turn them on, so this conserves power while leaving you ready to shoot on a moment's notice.

The LCD's position is also important. This is where it pays to buy a camera in a store (rather than online), since you can actually lay your hands on the model you are considering. Spend some time holding the camera and see where your hands tend to fall. If your natural hand position puts your thumb in the middle of the LCD, you are going to be spending a lot of time cleaning thumbprints off the screen.

Finally, check the brightness of the LCD. If you have to struggle to see the image because the LCD screen is too dim, look for another model. When trying out a camera in a store, look for some bright lights and check out what the screen looks like with a lot of light falling on it—glare can be a problem.

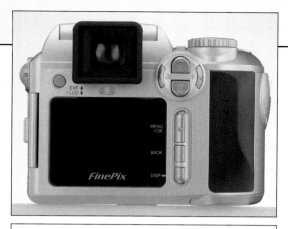

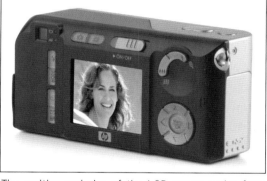

The position and size of the LCD screen varies from model to model.

■ VIEWFINDER

Digital cameras also come with a traditional type of viewfinder (the kind where you lift the camera to your eye and look into a little window). So why would you want to use this viewfinder instead of the fancy LCD screen? Well, as noted above, when light falls directly on the LCD screen, glare can make it hard to see your image. In that case, the viewfinder is a better option. Some people also just prefer to shoot the way they are used to shooting on their film cameras. When using the viewfinder, most cameras allow you to turn off the LCD screen completely—and that makes your batteries last longer. This is a good strategy to use when your batteries are running a bit low but you really want to keep shooting.

12. DIGITAL CAMERAS: LENSES

Every single picture you take will be made through whatever lens is on your camera, and that makes those curved pieces of glass pretty important. The type of lens on a digital camera tends to depend on the type of camera. In most cases (except for high-end cameras), digital cameras feature built-in lenses that can't be changed. This makes it important to determine the lens features you want before buying a new camera.

■ FIXED LENSES

Minicams and low-end point-and-shoot models often offer fixed lenses. This means that, when you look through the camera, there will be only one view of the scene.

■ ZOOM LENSES

Most point-and-shoot models feature a zoom lens. This type of lens lets you choose between several views of a scene. You can zoom in (use a telephoto setting) to get a closer view, or zoom out (use a wide-angle setting) to see a broader view. This gives you a lot more options when it comes to composing your photographs (see pages 36–37).

The power of a zoom lens (how tightly it can zoom in, how widely it can zoom out) is expressed as its focal length, measured in millimeters (e.g., 18–70mm). This is a way of describing how the lens will render a scene or subject on the image sensor. While the magnifying power of a given lens is constant, the lens may *function* differently depending on the size of the image-sensor chip in the camera—and this varies widely. If the focal length of the lens was calculated based on each model's unique chip size, this would make it hard to compare lenses from camera to camera. Therefore, manufacturers base their calculations of focal lengths on the size of a classic 35mm film frame. For this reason, it is often listed as the "effective focal length" (i.e., how it would work on a 35mm camera).

The power of the lens may also be listed as something like "4x," meaning that the most telephoto setting is four times greater than the most wide-angle setting. For example, an 18–70mm zoom lens could also be listed as a 3.8x zoom ($70 \div 18 = 3.8$).

Another specification you'll often see listed with lens data is optical (or actual) zoom vs. digital (or enhanced) zoom. The number you want to look at is the optical value. This is the amount of enlargement produced by the lens itself. "Digital zoom" is not really zoom at all—it's a software function that simply crops the image in the camera. This results in poor image quality. If you want to move in more tightly on a subject than you can with your lens, you're better off either moving your camera closer to the subject or, if that's not possible, cropping the image later on your computer where you have more control (see pages 62–63).

■ INTERCHANGEABLE LENSES

Most high-end cameras, like digital SLRs, employ lenses that can be removed and switched. You can select fixed focal-length lenses or zoom lenses, telephotos or wide-angles—whatever you want. The only drawback is that these systems can be very expensive. If you want the ultimate flexibility, however, it's definitely the best way to go!

OTHER LENS-RELATED CONCERNS

CLOSE FOCUSING

The close-focus setting lets you bring your lens to within a few inches of your subject and still get a well-focused shot. This makes it good for photographing small subjects, like flowers.

FILTER ADAPTERS

Filters attach to the lens of the camera (or, on some models, over the lens, using an accessory filter adapter) and allow you to adjust the light entering the camera in creative ways. You can add starbursts, remove glare, enhance color—and that's just the start! If you want the maximum in flexibility, therefore, look for a digital camera model that allows you to use filters—not all models do.

ACCESSORY LENSES

If your camera accepts filters, you may also be able to purchase a wide-angle or telephoto accessory lens to stretch the function of your built-in lens. The availability of these lenses isn't an excuse to skimp on zoom range when buying a camera (the image quality when using them usually isn't quite first-rate), but they can be very useful in a pinch!

13. DIGITAL CAMERAS: FLASH

Built-in flash has been on cameras for a long, long time, but most cameras gave you very little control over it. With digital, the controls are (at least on most models) significantly enhanced—and the LCD screen lets you make sure you've achieved the results you want.

■ AUTOMATIC VS. MANUAL

In the automatic mode, your camera chooses the amount of flash needed for a well-exposed image. If a scene seems well lit but your camera insists on using the flash, try finding a place to stabilize your camera and turn off the flash—you'll usually get better results. Or, if your camera offers manual settings, consult your user's guide. You may be able to reduce the flash output to better balance it with the other light in the scene and avoid some of the pitfalls of flash lighting (see below).

■ RED-EYE REDUCTION

Red-eye occurs when the lens and flash are directly in line with the subject's eyes. Most cameras now include red-eye reduction to prevent this. When it's

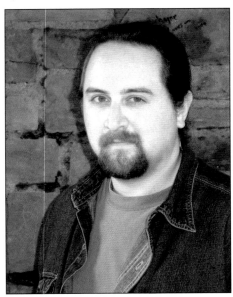 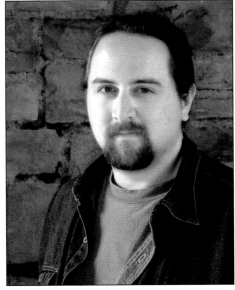

Images taken with on-camera flash as the main source of light in the photograph tend to have sharp shadows outlining one side of the subject (left). If there's enough light to use a longer exposure instead of the flash, you can usually create a more attractive shot (right). This may require a long shutter speed, so shooting from a tripod is a good idea.

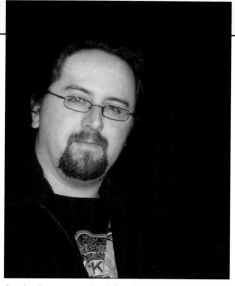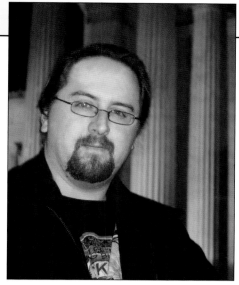

In the image on the left, the subject stands in front of the faintly illuminated columns of an art museum. The columns, however, are too distant for flash to do any good. The answer is the night portrait mode. In this mode, the subject is lit by the flash—but then the camera continues to expose the image, allowing the less intense light in the background to contribute more significantly to the final exposure. A tripod is strongly recommended when shooting in this mode (although you can get some interesting blur effects by quickly moving the camera immediately after the flash fires).

used, a short burst of light immediately precedes the flash with which the exposure is made. The initial burst closes down the pupil, preventing the flash from reflecting off the retina and back into the camera, which is what makes the center of the eye look red. If red-eye still occurs, you can fix it easily in your image-editing software (see page 67).

■ NIGHT PORTRAITS

The night portrait mode allows you to balance a dark background with a flash-lit foreground subject. See the images and caption above to learn how this works.

ON-CAMERA FLASH

On-camera flash only travels about 10 to 15 feet before it's too weak to make a good exposure. Therefore, if your subject is too far away, flash won't help. Conversely, flash is very intense close to the camera—so intense it can wash out too-close subjects. If your flash-lit subject's skin tones look pasty, take a few steps back and you'll usually get better results.

14. DIGITAL CAMERAS: SHUTTER CONTROLS

The shutter is what opens and allows light into the digital camera to make an exposure. When it opens and how long it is open (the shutter speed) are important concerns for getting a correct exposure and for freezing or blurring action.

■ SHUTTER LAG

One of the big problems with early digital cameras was that there was often a significant delay between when you pushed the shutter button and when the photo was actually taken. That made it really hard to take action shots! Today's cameras are a lot better, but there's usually still a tiny delay. Therefore, when timing your image is important, you'll want to try to anticipate the action and pop the shutter just before it peaks. Experience with your camera will make this a bit easier.

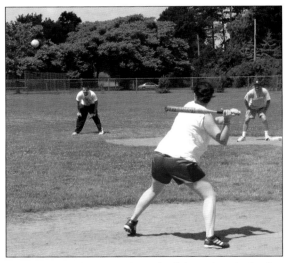

■ ACTION SEQUENCES

Most digital cameras offer a burst or continuous shooting mode (sometimes also called a sports or action mode). When you use this mode, your camera will keep taking images for as long as you hold down the shutter button (until either your memory card runs out of storage space or your camera runs out of processing memory and has to pause before shooting the next image).

If you click the shutter at the peak of the action, shutter lag can cause you to miss the moment. Instead, you need to anticipate the action and click the shutter just before it's about to happen.

This is great for fast action—but read your camera's manual closely. On some models, choosing this setting will automatically switch the camera to a lower resolution setting or a higher compression setting. This makes the files smaller so that more images can be processed but may leave you with too few pixels to make the size print you want of your best image.

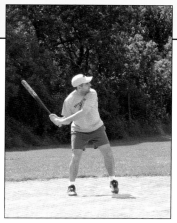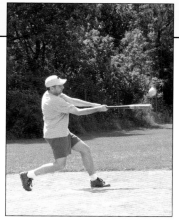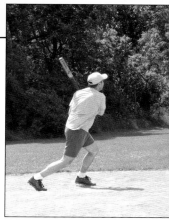

Using the burst or continuous-shooting mode creates a sequence of images, giving you better odds of capturing exactly the shot you want. Photos by Paul Grant.

■ SHUTTER SPEED

Here's (literally) the long and short of shutter speeds: when you choose a long shutter speed, subjects in motion will be blurred in your image; when you choose a short shutter speed, subjects in motion will be frozen in your image.

Look at the softball shots on these two pages. You'll see that the batters are all pretty much frozen in time. That's because a short shutter speed

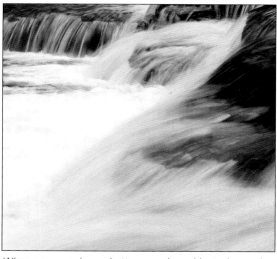

When you use long shutter speeds, subjects in motion become blurred.

was used. Now, look at the waterfall image above. Here, a long shutter speed was used to blur the motion.

■ REMOTE SHOOTING

Like most point-and-shoot film cameras, your digital will probably have a timer that allows you to set the camera and then duck into the shot. Depending on the model, your camera may also come with a remote control. This nifty device lets you stay in front of the camera and shoot as many images as you want.

15. DIGITAL CAMERAS: ADVICE FOR BUYING

No camera is the right one for every photographer—our needs and tastes are all too different. What's important is to figure out what you want, then find a model that fits those needs. Here are some things to consider:

1. **Megapixels**—How big do you want to be able to make prints?
2. **Lens**—Do you need a lot of zoom or just a little? Or would a camera with interchangeable lenses fit your needs better?
3. **Special Features**—Do you like to take pictures at your daughter's soccer games? If so, make sure there's a continuous shooting mode. Do you love taking landscape photos? If so, you'll probably want a panoramic mode as well as a landscape setting. Maybe close-ups of flowers suit your fancy—which means you'll want to be sure there's a macro or close-up mode.
4. **Memory Card**—If this is your second digital camera (or someone else in your household has one), consider sticking with a model that uses the same memory card format so you don't have to buy new media.
5. **Cost**—Know your budget. Don't break yourself to get features you don't even need (equally, don't skimp and pass up on things you want just to save twenty bucks).

You may want to rank the qualities you are looking for as "needs" and "wants." When you're shopping, you'll only want to look at models that have all your needs—then you can concentrate on finding cameras that have as many of your wants as possible.

You may want to rank the qualities you are looking for as "needs" and "wants."

Finally, take the time to do your homework. Spend an evening online narrowing down the models you are interested in and reading reviews (some resources for this are listed on the facing page). Talk to the folks at your local camera shop and see what their experiences have been and what they recommend (and, if possible, support them by buying locally instead of online).

You probably also have friends who already own digital cameras. Ask them what they love (or hate) about theirs. It can be very revealing—they may have had problems or discovered advantages you'd never think of!

RESOURCES

Before you buy, check out some of these helpful resources. Visit the manufacturer's web site for a complete list of specifications, but also be sure to read some reviews on other sites.

CAMERA MANUFACTURERS

Canon—www.canon.com
Casio—www.casio.com
Contax—www.kyoceraimaging.com
Fuji—www.fujifilm.com
Hewlett-Packard—
    www.hewlett-packard.com
JVC—www.jvc.com
Kodak—www.kodak.com
Leica—www.leica-camera.com
Nikon—www.nikon.com
Olympus—www.olympus.com
Panasonic—www.panasonic.com
Pentax—www.pentax.com
Polaroid—www.polaroid.com
Samsung—www.samsung.com
Sanyo—www.sanyo.com
Sony—www.sony.com
Toshiba—www.toshiba.com
Vivitar—www.vivitar.com

MEDIA REVIEWS

c|net—www.cnet.com
Consumer Reports—
    www.consumerreports.org
Digital Camera magazine—
    www.digicamera.com
Digital Camera Resource Page—
    www.dcresource.com

Digital Camera Review Spot—
    www.digitalcamerareviewspot.com
Digital Photographer magazine—
    www.digiphotomag.com
Digital Photography Review—
    www.dpreview.com
ePhotozine—www.ephotozine.com
Imaging Resource—
    www.imaging-resource.com
pcphoto review—
    www.pcphotoreview.com
Photo Techniques magazine—
    www.phototechmag.com
Popular Photography magazine—
    www.popularphotography.com
Shutterbug magazine—
    www.shutterbug.com
Steve's Digicams—
    www.steves-digicams.com

USER REVIEWS

Amazon—www.amazon.com
Ask an Owner—
    www.askanowner.com
Camera Forums—
    www.cameraforums.net
Digital Camera HQ—
    www.digitalcamera-hq.com
Epinions—www.epinions.com

16. DIGITAL CAMERAS: COMPOSITION

Composition is the term used to describe the conscious placement of subjects within the frame. Believe it or not, more than any other quality, composition can make or break a photograph. Let's start with what *not* to do.

■ WHAT TO AVOID

The most boring composition is one where you center your subject in the frame. This "bull's-eye" type of composition is very static and doesn't encourage the viewer's eyes to linger on the frame. Placing your subject off center instead makes the viewer's eyes travel around the image, evaluating the main subject and the areas around it—which is just the reaction you want!

You should also look to eliminate potential distractions. For example, our eyes are drawn to areas of contrast in a frame. Imagine you have photographed a scene of rolling green hills. Now imagine that there is one tree on one hill with red leaves. Where are your eyes going to be drawn? Directly to that single red tree.

Another common problem is getting so wrapped up with the subject of your image that you miss seeing distractions at the edges. A common one is a branch sticking into the edge of the image.

COMPOSITION TIPS

1. **Use the LCD Screen.** Composing on the LCD screen usually makes it easier to imagine what your print will look like—and any problems seem a bit more obvious.

2. **Try Some Variations.** Rarely is your first idea about how to compose a scene the best one. Try out some variations—remember, with digital, it doesn't cost you a cent!

3. **Zoom In, Zoom Out.** If your camera has a zoom lens, try starting with a wide-angle setting, then begin zooming in to pick out just what's important. Often, compositions fail because they include too much. Try to eliminate anything that doesn't help tell the story you want your viewer to see in your image.

4. **Don't Forget Verticals.** Most photos are taken as horizontals, because that's how we tend to hold our cameras. Many subjects, however, work much better in vertical compositions, so don't be lazy—tip your camera on end for a few shots!

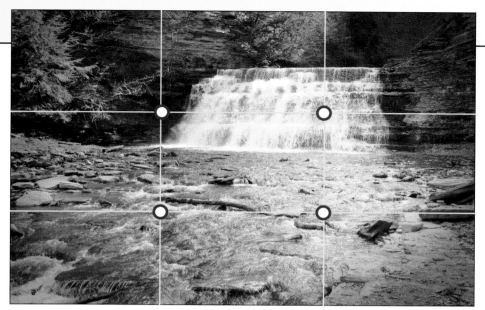

Composing according to the rule of thirds creates more dynamic images. Here, it gives the water room to flow diagonally through the frame, drawing your eye along with it.

■ THE RULE OF THIRDS

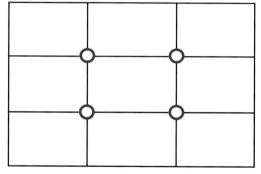

The rule of thirds is a formula used by photographers, painters, and other artists as a guideline for determining a strong place to position their subject within the frame. According to the rule of thirds, the image frame is divided into thirds (like a tic-tac-toe board). This is shown in the diagram above. Subjects can be successfully placed along any of these lines, and may be emphasized by placing them at the intersection of any two lines (these intersections are sometimes called "power points"). Whether your image is horizontal or vertical, this guideline applies in exactly the same way.

When using image-editing software to crop your images (see pages 62–63), you should also keep the rule of thirds in mind, since cropping can change the composition, depending on how you do it.

Note that this is not a hard-and-fast rule. Your subject and aesthetic sensibilities will ultimately determine the best composition for each image, but the rule of thirds provides a good place to start and will help you remember to avoid centering the subject.

17. DIGITAL CAMERAS: EXPOSURE

If you're accustomed to shooting print film, you'll need to adjust your normal exposure techniques somewhat as you make the leap to digital. With print film, you meter and expose for the shadows, ensuring detail in the darkest area of your image. Print film is great at holding detail in bright highlights, so these areas become a secondary consideration. Print films are also very forgiving, so the exposure can be significantly off from the "perfect" exposure and still be usable.

With digital, you expose and meter for the highlights, and your exposure must be more precise to produce a usable image. This is because digital has an annoying tendency to "blow out" (render as pure, bald white with no detail) the bright highlight areas in a scene. The results can be really unattractive.

If this sounds foreboding, don't worry—there are a lot of great things about digital that, ultimately, make it easier to get a well-exposed image than ever before.

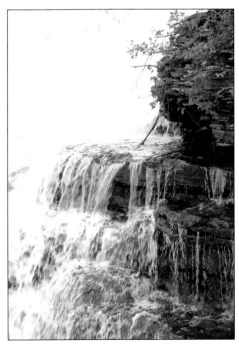 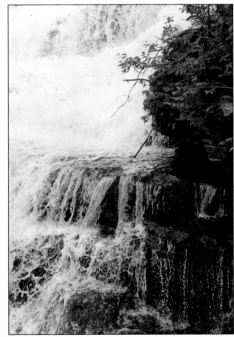

For the image on the left, the exposure was metered off a dark area on the rocks. This rendered the stones well, but the waterfall is so lacking in detail that it's almost impossible to even identify. On the right, the exposure was metered off the water, producing an exposure that better retained detail in this area. The rocks may be a little dark (depending on your tastes), but they could be lightened using your image-editing software.

READING HISTOGRAMS

Most digital cameras allow you to view what's called a "histogram" for each image you shoot. Using this graphic representation of the tones in your image, it's easy to get a good idea of where there might be problems.

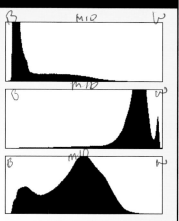

Here's the idea: in the histogram, the tones in the image are broken down into data that is represented in a diagram from left (pure black) to right (pure white). Tones in the middle area are called "midtones" (somewhere between black and white). The taller the jagged black data is over a given area of this black-to-white scale, the more tones in the image fall into that range. For example, in the first histogram (top) most of the tones are to the far left. This tells you that most of the image is very dark. In the second example (center), most of the data is over the light areas, telling you that the image is mostly very light. In the final example (bottom), we see a more typical arrangement—some light, some dark, but most tones somewhere in the middle.

The histogram will be different for each image—and there's no "right" histogram. What you should look for in terms of exposure, however, is a histogram that tapers down toward the ends (even if steeply) and doesn't crowd up over the pure white or pure black points (the extreme ends). This can be a sign of loss of detail in either the highlights or the shadows.

The process is really just this simple: meter for the brightest important part of your scene, then shoot your picture. In the image-review mode, examine the highlights carefully. Many cameras let you zoom in on the image to see more detail. Because blown-out highlights are a known issue with digital, many cameras let you review your images in a mode where areas of pure white with no detail blink in the preview. Other cameras let you look at a histogram of the image (see above).

If you spot a problem with the highlights, reshoot the image at a faster shutter speed or smaller aperture. Many cameras also offer exposure compensation controls; if you are shooting in the auto mode, using this feature is a good way to reduce the exposure of the image to control the highlights.

18. DIGITAL CAMERAS: FOCUSING

Focus is a big issue for photographers. Shooting digitally, however, puts some very sophisticated tools at our fingertips to ensure we can keep our images sharp.

■ AUTOFOCUS

The autofocus systems on today's cameras are extremely sophisticated and provide great results for most scenes. There are still a few things that can trip them up, though. These include very low contrast subjects, scenes that mix close and far objects, scenes with extremely bright subjects at the center of the composition, and quickly moving subjects.

■ FOCUS LOCK

Many of the aforementioned problems can be solved using focus lock. To do

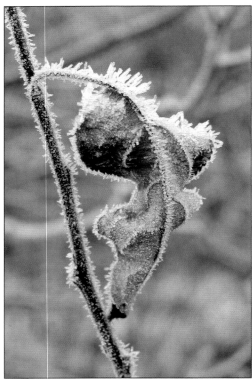

The macro setting on a point-and-shoot camera lets you get up quite close to small subjects and still keep them in focus.

this, aim your camera at a second subject that is the same distance from the camera as the intended subject. Focus on this and press the shutter button halfway down to lock the focus setting. Keep the shutter button half pressed, then re-compose the image and shoot.

■ MANUAL FOCUS

For tricky subjects, try manual focus. On a point-and-shoot camera (if it's offered), the manual focus can be a bit tricky, so consult your user's guide for tips and evaluate each shot carefully to ensure that you have focused correctly. On a digital SLR, simply switch to manual focus mode and adjust the focusing ring on your lens until the focus indicator shows that the image is correctly focused.

■ ADVANCED FEATURES

Many SLRs now offer really advanced focusing features that allow you to quickly adjust the focus to a subject that is off center or even to automatically track a moving subject and retain focus. If your camera offers these features, learn how they work and put them to use!

As noted on page 40, many cameras also allow for close focusing—making it possible to take sharp images even when your lens is only a few inches from the subject.

■ CHECKING THE FOCUS

After you shoot an image,

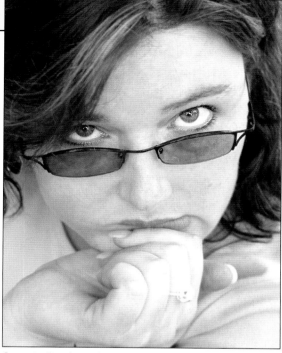

In portraits, the main area to concern yourself with is the eyes. If those are sharp, the focus elsewhere in the portrait almost doesn't matter. If you want a contemporary feel, letting almost everything but the eyes go slightly out of focus creates a very appealing look.

preview it on the LCD screen and (if your camera allows) zoom in on the most important element in the frame to make sure that it's sharp. In a portrait, this is usually the subject's eyes. If the eyes are not sharp, reshoot the image—and be thankful you found out about the problem while there was still a chance to correct it!

■ SHARPENING

If your focus is close but not quite perfect, most digital-imaging software can help you to improve it. See pages 68–69 for more on this.

MORE ON FOCUS

Of course, totally sharp focus isn't right for every image; for some shots, you may want to use blurring to show that the subject is in motion or to make the image look jittery. As the artist, the choice is yours!

19. DIGITAL CAMERAS: IMAGE MODES

Most digital cameras offer a range of features that were not options on film cameras. If you know how to use these settings, they can help you create better images. The following are some of the most common options.

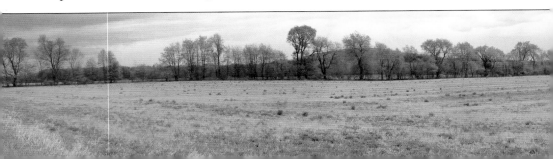

■ AUTO

Usually indicated by "auto" on the image mode dial or menu, in this mode the camera makes all the decisions for you. With today's sophisticated metering systems, this often provides a very good exposure.

On most models, the image modes are selected from a dial on the top of the camera. On others, these options are selected from on-screen menus.

■ PROGRAM

The program mode (usually indicated by a "P") is similar to the auto mode but it usually allows you to exercise control over some camera settings (like white balance, ISO, etc.).

■ SHUTTER PRIORITY

In this mode (commonly indicated by "Tv"), you select the shutter speed and the camera selects the best aperture for the brightness of the scene. Choose a short shutter speed to freeze moving subjects or a long one to blur them.

■ APERTURE PRIORITY

This mode is usually denoted by an "Av" on the exposure dial or menu. It allows you to select the aperture while the camera sets the shutter speed.

■ MANUAL

In this mode (indicated by "M"), you control all the settings, giving you complete control over the exposure.

■ PORTRAIT

In the portrait mode (indicated by a profile of a face), the camera selects a wide aperture to keep the subject in focus while blurring the background.

■ LANDSCAPE

In the landscape mode (usually indicated by a mountain and clouds icon), a narrow aperture is selected to keep as much as possible of the scene in focus. This mode works well for vast landscape scenes.

■ NIGHT PORTRAIT

The night portrait mode, usually denoted by a profile of a face with a moon and stars next to it, is used to take a well-exposed image of a subject against a night scene. For more on this, see page 31.

■ ARTISTIC EFFECTS

Often indicated by a palette and brush, this mode allows you to select from color options that may include shooting in black & white or sepia-toned as well as vivid color (enhanced color saturation and contrast) or neutral color (subdued color saturation and contrast).

■ PANORAMIC MODE

In the panoramic mode, the camera helps you to create a series of slightly overlapping shots that can later be combined into one big, long image using image-stitching software (see page 58). An example of such an image is shown below.

■ CONTINUOUS

This mode is normally indicated by a stack of rectangles (photos) and lets you shoot successive frames for as long as the shutter button is pressed (until the camera or memory card runs out of memory).

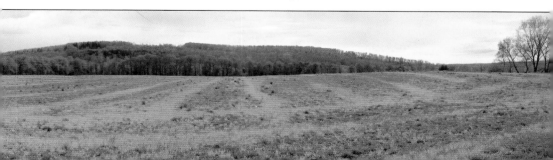

20. SCANNING: THE BASICS

Even if you've totally embraced digital photography, the reality is that the vast majority of the images taken in the history of photography were taken on film (or some other non-digital medium). Your parents' and grandparents' wedding pictures, family baby pictures, photos from long-past vacations—all of these mean that film is still going to be with us for quite a while. Who'd want to give up on these treasures?

The good news is that, with a scanner, you can enjoy and share these images more easily than ever. You can also restore them to their original condition—something that would have been incredibly expensive before digital imaging came around.

Of course, a scanner is also great if you still want to use a film camera but get the benefits of digital imaging.

■ TYPES OF SCANNERS

There are two basic types of scanners: one to digitize prints and one to digitize slides and negatives.

Print scanners are often called flatbed scanners, because you place the print on a flat glass bed. With the image in place, an image sensor with a light unit attached to it moves beneath the glass and "reads" the photograph. Electronics then translate the data from the sensors into an image.

Transparency scanners are more expensive than flatbed scanners. However, because slides and negatives hold image detail better than prints, they also offer better quality. The two types of scanners work in much the same way—but with a transparency scanner, the light source is on one side of the film or slide and the image sensor is on the other (i.e., the light shines through the film and hits the image sensor).

Some scanners can digitize prints and transparent media. These look like flatbeds but also have a built-in adapter to hold slides

GETTING CREATIVE

Prints aren't the only thing you can scan on your flatbed scanner—anything flat will work. You can experiment leaves, flowers, decorative paper, fabric, etc. Just be sure not to place any object on the scanner glass that could scratch it!

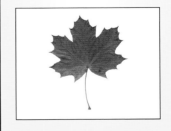

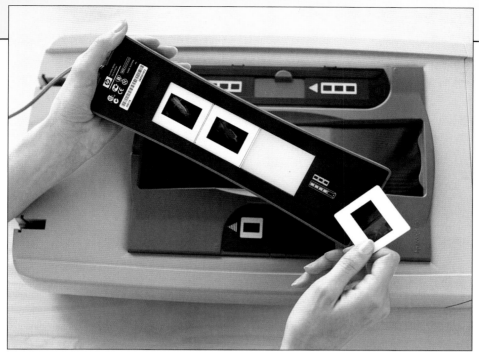

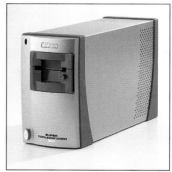

Some flatbed scanners (above) offer an adapter that allows you to scan transparent media. This feature usually costs a little bit more, but it may be worth it to you if you have a lot of slides or negatives in your image collection. Transparency scanners (right) create digital files from slides and negatives. When buying, keep in mind the format of the images you want to scan. If you have non-35mm media (like large-format film, or negatives from antique cameras), you may need to purchase a special unit or an adapter. Some scanners accept only one format.

and negatives, as well as a light to shine through these media and onto the image sensor. If you have a variety of media to scan, this can be a good choice.

■ RESOLUTION AND BIT DEPTH

The resolution of a scanner tells you how much data can be recorded by the image sensor. Look for the optical resolution; this is the data that the scanner can actually capture without software enhancements. The bit depth tells you how well it can differentiate between shades of colors. Most models provide overall good results for photography; really expensive models sometimes offer more bit depth, which can be good for high-contrast prints and slides.

21. SCANNING: PREPARING TO SCAN

In scanning, an ounce of prevention during the input process will be much better than a pound of cure. Correcting a poorly scanned image is rarely worth your time (and it's almost never 100 percent successful). It makes sense to select the best input method in the first place and make every effort to avoid preventable flaws in the scanned image.

■ DUST

One very common, very preventable flaw is dust on the surface of the image. When scanning prints, invest in some dust-free cloths and wipe down the scanner glass and the surface of the image before every scan. For slides and negatives, use an antistatic brush and compressed air. While dust on prints can be pretty annoying, dust on slides and negatives can be a huge problem. Since the originals start out so small, when you enlarge your scan to the size needed to make a print (say, 8"x10"), you'll enlarge any dust particles along with the rest of the image data. A large spot of dust on a slide can actually obscure a significant area of the image!

Wipe down the scanner glass and the surface of the image before every scan.

Software is available to help correct for dust in scans (because, despite your best efforts, there will usually still be a spot or two). Adobe Photoshop Elements, for example, offers a Dust & Scratches filter to help eliminate problems. This does indeed work, but there can be a trade-off in image quality, so use such tools cautiously.

■ RESOLUTION

Another problem can be solved with a little extra attention to detail. Sooner or later you'll scan an image, spend hours perfecting it, and then realize you had the scanner set at too low a resolution. No matter how many times you've used the software, it pays to take a moment before each scan to review the settings to make sure you'll get what you want. For more on this, see page 48.

■ A GOOD ORIGINAL

Finally, while the world of digital imaging offers many opportunities to correct flaws in images, you'll still be happiest when you start with the best-

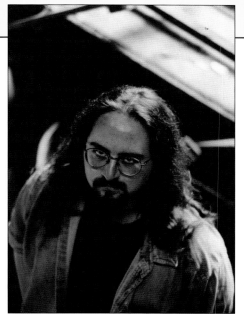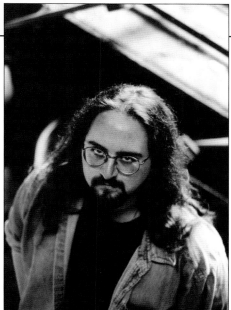

Auto scanner settings are sometimes problematic (left). Using custom settings can often improve your scan (right).

possible original. Sometimes there isn't a good original to scan (often, that's why we're scanning it to begin with). But, if you have a choice between two versions of the same image, scan the best one.

In general, it is easier to darken an image than to lighten one. When you start with a dark image and try to lighten it, you usually end up with shadow areas that are off color and too grainy. Therefore, if you have to choose between a slightly underexposed (dark) original and a slightly overexposed (light) original, you'll usually want to go with the overexposure. (If, however, the image is so light that there is no detail in the highlights, you'll still have a problem because there may not be any detail present to darken.)

■ TRY AGAIN

Finally, don't forget that you can always re-scan. When the first scan comes up on your screen, take a good look at it. Check out the resolution and examine the highlight and shadow areas to see if the detail you want has been captured. If you're not convinced it's the best scan you can get with your equipment, try again. Scanning is an art, and the more you use your equipment, the better you'll get at anticipating the results.

22. SCANNING: MAKING A GOOD SCAN

A lot of things have to go right to create a really top-quality scan—but most of them are pretty easy to figure out based on what you want to do with your image.

■ DETERMINE THE END USE

Before you even get started, you need to know how you want to use the scan you're about to create. Do you just want to e-mail a photo to a friend or put it up on a web page? Do you want to get a print made—and if so, how big do you want it to be? Will you be running the image in a newsletter? Or maybe you're planning to create a huge poster? The file you need to create will be different depending on the output you want.

■ SELECT THE RIGHT RESOLUTION

Once you know how you want to use your image, you should be able to figure out what the resolution needs to be. For e-mailing or web-page viewing, 72dpi will do the job. To make a print at a lab, you'll probably need about 200dpi. To print your image in a color newsletter or as a poster, you might need 300dpi. If you will be printing the image yourself at home, consult your printer's manual to see what it recommends you use; if you'll be having the image printed professionally, ask the lab or print provider for their exact specifications.

> With slides and negatives, you'll almost always want to enlarge the image from the original.

■ SELECT THE SCALE

With slides and negatives, you'll almost always want to enlarge the image from the original (unless, perhaps, you are designing a postage stamp). With prints, too, the whole reason for scanning them may be to get a larger picture from an image when the negative has been lost. Let's imagine you are starting with a 4"x5" print and you want to make an 8"x10" print. How much would you need to enlarge it? Well, you want to double the size, so you'd set the enlargement to 200 percent. For a 5"x7", you'd set it to 140 percent, etc. If this seems confusing, see if your scanner software lets you specify a "target," "final," or "page" size—then you can just type in the dimensions you want the final image to be.

■ OTHER SETTINGS

Most scanners also allow you to choose from additional settings. For example, you may be able to sharpen your images. Most scans do need a little sharpening, so this can be a good thing. Try it out and see if you're happy with the results. (You can also sharpen your images using your image-editing software, a method that provides much greater control—see pages 68–69 for more information on this.)

You may also be able to specify whether you want to create a color or black & white scan. How you decide to set this will depend on your original image. If your original is black & white, you may want to select the grayscale setting. If your image is in color, keep in mind that you can always convert it to black & white later on using your image-editing software, but you can't really go the other way.

Most scanners also give you some color and tonal adjustment tools. These vary widely by model, so check your manual to see if these tools will work for you and enhance your results.

■ CHECK THE SETTINGS

When you're doing a series of identical scans, it's easy to forget to check the software settings, but it pays to do it every time. If you don't, you'll eventually discover that the resolution got set back to 72dpi, or the scale is wrong, or something. That can be one incredibly frustrating experience!

CALLING IN THE PROFESSIONALS

Scanning, as you have probably figured out, can be pretty time consuming, and getting the best-possible results requires good equipment and some experience. For this reason, professional scanning can be useful—especially when you have a lot of images to scan (like a whole slide collection). Professional scans, returned to you on CD, can be obtained at most photo labs (even some mini-labs in grocery and drugstores now offer them). You can even drop your exposed film off for processing and get back both prints and a CD. For high-end needs, there are top-quality scanning service providers all over the country (and the world, for that matter) whose experienced technicians know how to draw the best out of every image. Check out the prices at different suppliers; they can vary widely.

23. HARDWARE: COMPUTERS

In the world of digital photography, your computer plays a central role. Without it, you couldn't really take advantage of all the great opportunities digital imaging affords. The good news is that the same computer you use to read your e-mail, write sales reports, and buy books online will probably work just fine. The following are some tips for ensuring you have what you need.

■ PLATFORM

Does it matter if you work on a PC or a Mac? Although users of one system or the other may have their personal loyalties to their platform of choice, it really doesn't matter that much. What's more important is that the system you use has the speed, memory, and other qualities that make it efficient and reliable to use—and, above all, that you are comfortable using it.

■ SPEED

Manipulating an image requires your computer to do a lot of fancy math—so you'll want to make sure it can do so quickly. Unfortunately, getting the real low-down on this can be tricky since the methods used to calculate speed vary and make clock-speed comparisons irrelevant. The best approach is to check out the software you want to run and make sure the computer you own

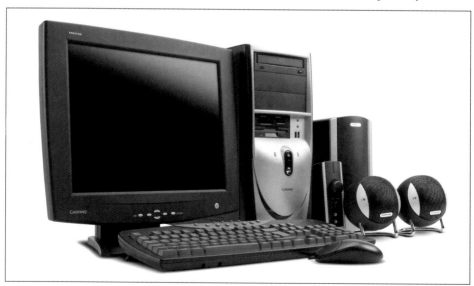

Windows-based PCs are popular in the business world, so they are many people's first choice when purchasing a home computer.

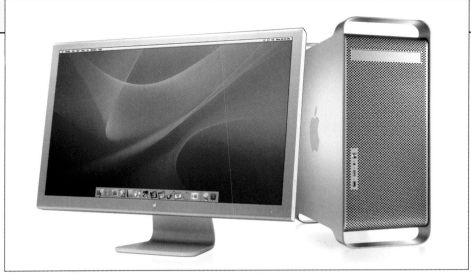

Macintosh computers tend to be favored by students and professionals who work in creative fields like photography and graphic design.

(or plan to buy) has sufficient speed. Most current systems are more than adequate.

■ MEMORY

RAM. This is the memory your software and images are loaded into when you open them. If you have too little, things will get really slow. Again, check your software to determine its minimum requirements—and add more RAM if you need to (it's actually quite cheap!).

Hard Drive. A big hard drive is ideal, since image files can take up lots of space. Something in the 60GB to 80GB range is great, but you can get away with less if you need to.

DIGITAL PHOTOGRAPHY ON THE GO

How many memory cards do you really want to buy? For long photography expeditions, a laptop will serve you well. In addition to giving you a quick way to upload your photos, you can use the laptop's CD/DVD burner to make daily backups of vacation photos—and get online to e-mail pictures back home.

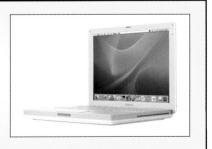

24. HARDWARE: MONITORS

Your monitor is the primary visual component of your computer. If, like many who get into digital photography, you become semi-obsessed with refining your images, you're going to spend a lot of time looking at it.

■ COLOR AND QUALITY

One of the primary concerns when it comes to selecting a monitor is how well it represents color. This is obviously more important for digital photography than for, say, word processing. In addition, you should consider the quality of the picture. It's especially important to check the edges of the viewing area to see if the image looks fuzzy or distorted. If so, move on to another model.

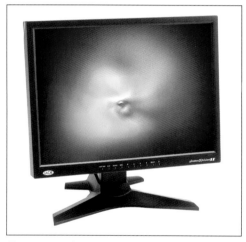

Flat-screen LCD monitors are the latest in viewing technology. They offer some advantages but still come with a pretty steep price tag.

■ SIZE

Monitors increase exponentially in price as they get bigger. For most people, a 17-inch monitor is about the smallest that is comfortable for digital imaging. In part, this is due to the fact that most image-editing programs feature many screen-area-consuming palettes that reduce the amount of viewing space for your image.

Also, with CRT models (see facing page), a "17-inch monitor" may not actually have 17 inches of viewing area; the viewable area may be one to two inches smaller. Most specifications for monitors list the viewable area, so look for this listing.

If you can afford it, a really big monitor is great—but be aware that really big monitors require really big desks!

■ RESOLUTION

Virtually every monitor can support 640x480-pixel resolution (also called "VGA" resolution). To display more information on the screen, most also offer at least one "Super VGA" setting—often 800x600 or 1600x1280 pixels. High-end monitors offer even higher resolutions.

■ REFRESH RATE

High refresh rates (or, on LCDs, pixel response times) help reduce screen flicker, which in turn reduces eye strain and (in some people) headaches.

■ DOT PITCH

This measurement is used to determine how sharp the display of a CRT monitor is. The smaller the number, the finer the picture. Most monitors have a dot pitch between

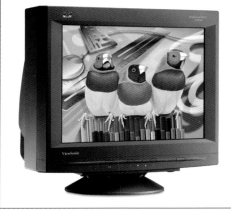

CRT (Cathode Ray Tube) monitors are the most common type. Although their prices are pretty friendly, they do have some drawbacks—one of which is their sheer size, which can eat up a whole lot of desk space.

.25mm and .28mm. On a very large monitor, a higher dot pitch (in the .30mm range) will still produce a pleasantly crisp image.

LCD OR CRT?

CRT monitors are the most popular type on the market, but LCDs are gaining ground. What's holding people back? Probably the price; LCDs are still a lot more expensive than CRT monitors of the same size. There are, however, benefits to LCDs, so as prices drop, they will likely become more popular.

First, LCD monitors take up a lot less space and are much easier to move. A big CRT can weigh 100 pounds while its LCD counterpart will check in at something under fifteen. LCDs also require less power—which in a time of rising electric bills is an important consideration. The flat, nonreflective screen of the LCD reduces eye strain. Low-end CRT models take a double hit on this count; their curved, shiny screens can make glare and distortion a real problem. (High-end CRTs do offer nearly flat screens that reduce glare and distortion, however.) LCDs also offer good color fidelity and a larger on-screen viewable area.

Are there problems? Sure. LCDs have lower refresh rates than CRTs (although this will change as the technology evolves). They also tend to have lower resolutions than CRTs. You should also watch out for "dead" pixels—dots on the screen that stop responding. Make sure this problem is covered by your monitor's warranty.

25. HARDWARE: USEFUL ADDITIONS

Once you've set up a computer with some kind of image-editing software, you can certainly leave it at that. If you want to spend a little more to add functionality and make your life a bit easier, the following are some good investments.

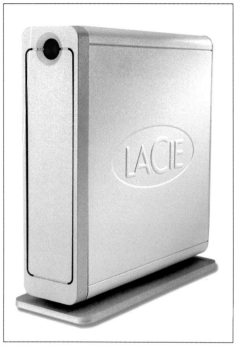

External hard drives are now quite reasonably priced and can add a lot of extra storage space to your computer system.

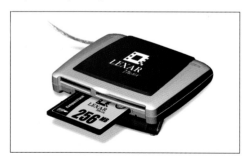

For many people, using a card reader to transfer images from their digital camera to their computer is a lot easier than having to attach the camera to the computer with a cable each time.

■ EXTRA STORAGE SPACE

Digital photographers tend to take a lot of pictures. Depending on the size of your computer's hard drive(s) and how much you shoot, you may need a little extra real estate to store your images. Adding an external hard drive can create that space. It is especially convenient for archiving images that you want close at hand. You should still back up your images to CD/DVD, of course; hard drives do crash from time to time.

■ CARD READERS

Most cameras allow you to upload your images by connecting your camera to your computer via a cable. Many people find it's actually easier, though, to use a card reader. Simply pop your memory card out of the camera and into the card reader and copy the files from the card onto your hard drive. Most card readers connect via a USB or FireWire port. When buying, you should also make sure that the reader you select is designed for the format of card you use. Some readers accept only one type; others are designed for multi-format use.

GRAPHICS TABLET

For really detailed image retouching, most people find it hard to get the level of precision they want with a regular mouse. The graphics tablet allows you to move your cursor around using a pen-shaped stylus—essentially allowing you to "draw" on the screen. Graphics tablets are also pressure sensitive—as with a real pen or paintbrush, pressing harder creates a wide, dark line; light pressure creates a thin, light line.

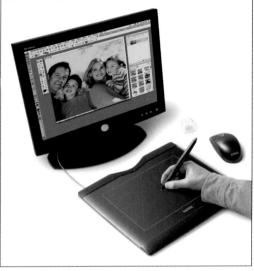

Using a graphics tablet lets you control your cursor more precisely than with a mouse—a great asset for detailed image retouching.

CD/DVD BURNER

This is really a necessity—but if you have an older computer with a slow CD burner, you might want to consider adding a faster one or even a DVD burner. You'll be making a lot of backup discs, so it makes sense to create them quickly and efficiently.

INTERNET CONNECTION

The Internet is a great source of information on digital imaging—including product reviews, tips, techniques, user forums, and more. You can also download updates and plug-ins for your digital-imaging software. Additionally, an Internet connection allows you to connect to online labs to print your photographs or set up digital albums. You can also use your connection to e-mail photos to your friends and family.

PRINTER

While printing at a lab is cheaper and produces better results, a good inkjet printer is a nice thing to have for quick prints, adding photos to letters, and other day-to-day tasks.

26. SOFTWARE: ALL PURPOSE

There are dozens of image-editing programs on the market. These allow you to crop, enhance, adjust, and otherwise alter your images. The following are some popular choices. All sell for less than $100—some *much* less.

■ ADOBE PHOTOSHOP ELEMENTS

Elements is a great bargain actually, giving you all but the most professional-level tools found in Adobe Photoshop (its big brother) but for about $500 less. Packed with powerful tools for retouching images, creating panoramics, adjusting color and exposure, adding special effects, and more, Elements is a great multipurpose image-editing tool. To learn more, visit www.adobe.com.

■ ROXIO PHOTOSUITE

PhotoSuite offers tools for correcting common photo problems and adding creative effects. Additionally, you can create slide shows with special transitions between images, music, and narration. A tool is also offered for fixing multiple photos at the same time. To learn more, just go to www.roxio.com.

■ ULEAD PHOTOIMPACT

PhotoImpact allows for the correction of common problems. You can also add artistic effects, text, graphics, and painting. This software provides many tools for using images on the Internet and the ability to design interactive digital photo slide shows. For more information, visit www.ulead.com.

■ HIJAAK DIGITAL PHOTO STUDIO

Digital Photo Studio walks you step-by-step through common tasks and performs all the functions you'd expect (cropping, exposure and color correction, special effects, etc.). To learn more, visit www.hijaak.com.

■ MICROSOFT PICTUREIT!

PictureIt! features quick tools for enhancing lighting, correcting the color and composition of your images, and restoring old photos. The "MiniLab" allows you to correct batches of photos at the same time. Pre-created templates (1500 of them!) are included to help you put your photos to good use in cards, frames, calendars, and other photo projects. For further information, visit www.microsoft.com/products/imaging.

■ JASC PAINT SHOP PRO

Paint Shop Pro offers a complete, all-around image-editing package that's just about on par with Adobe Photoshop Elements (although fewer books and supporting materials are available for learning it). For more information, visit www.jasc.com.

■ KAI'S PHOTO SOAP

Photo Soap is a quirky program with a totally unique interface that you'll either love or hate. It's hard to beat the price, though, for a program that lets you correct all the common problems, add special effects, create photo projects, organize your photos, and more. For additional information on this product, visit www.scansoft.com/photosoap.

■ ACDSEE

ACDSee provides automated and manual tools for enhanced control over your photographs. It's a very popular program with lots of loyal users. For more details, visit www.acdsystems.com.

■ PICTURE WINDOW PRO

Produced by Digital Light and Color, Picture Window Pro offers a comprehensive set of image-editing tools for photographers. Useful software is also included to help you create digital photo albums. For additional information, see www.dl-c.com.

TRY IT OUT

Even low-cost image-editing software isn't a bargain if it doesn't do what you want it to or has an awkward interface that you don't enjoy using. Rather than just buying the software off the shelf, it's a good idea to check out the manufacturer's web site. There, you'll find much more extensive detail than on the product packaging—and you may even find a trial version you can download and test out. Usually, these trial versions have all the features of the full version, but they don't allow you to save your work. They are also set to expire (cease to function) after a certain number of days or uses. This is a great way to get a sense of whether or not the product is worth your money.

27. SOFTWARE: SPECIALIZED

Check out any big software store and you'll see the shelves covered with hundreds of software products designed to make your images prettier, turn them into greeting cards, group them into interactive albums, set them to music, share them online, and much, much more. The following are some common types of specialized software.

■ IMAGE STITCHING

Several programs are available to help you turn a sequence of individual images into one gigantic one. PhotoVista Panorama from iseemedia (www.iseemedia. com) is one such program; its sole function is the creation of panoramic images. PhotoVista 3D, also from iseemedia, works on a similar principle, except it allows you to create a sequence of images that show a subject from all angles, then combine them into a 3-D image of the object that you can pick up and rotate on screen.

■ DIGITAL ALBUMS

One of the most popular types of digital-imaging software allows you to create virtual "albums" to be viewed on screen or printed out. Some even let you

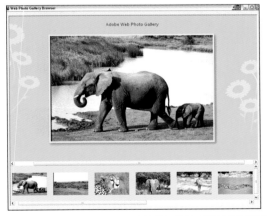

create a DVD of your album that will play on your home theater system. Adobe Photoshop Album (www.adobe.com) is popular, as is Flip Album (www.flipalbum.com).

Adobe Photoshop Album (left) lets you create web albums using predesigned page templates. Image stitching software seamlessly blends a series of individual images into one big one (below).

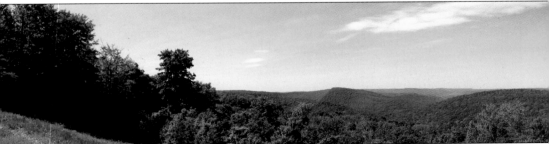

■ GREETING CARDS

There's a whole lot of greeting-card software on the market, so if you're interested in making your own, you're sure to find a product that suits your needs. Packages of templates are available for funny cards, inspirational cards, all-purpose cards, etc. Nova Development (www.novadevelopment.com) has several packages.

■ SPECIAL EFFECTS

Some programs are devoted to producing special effects. A good example of this is Kai's SuperGoo (www.scansoft.com). This nifty program actually "liquifies" your photograph and allows you to smear, warp, and stretch it as you like. You can even create an animated movie of the process—or add fake hair, eyes, noses, and more to your subjects from a library of facial components.

■ CALENDARS

Some of the programs used to create cards also let you make calendars using your own photographs—and these make great gifts for your friends and family! Print Shop Deluxe (www.Broderbund.com) is one such program. It includes thousands of templates for a variety of projects.

■ IMAGE ENLARGEMENT

Programs like Extensis pxl SmartScale (www.extensis.com) allow you to greatly increase the size of your images without any visible loss of quality.

■ SHARPENING

Sharpener Pro from nik Multimedia lets you sharpen your images while tailoring your results to your intended method of output—whether you use your images online, with an inkjet printer, or in a fine-art book. For more information, visit www.nikmultimedia.com.

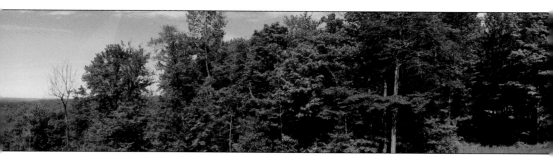

28. SOFTWARE: PLUG-INS

There are literally thousands of plug-ins on the market, yet most digital photography enthusiasts have never even heard of them! Once you scratch the surface, you can quickly get hooked on the neat little programs (which also, thankfully, tend to be inexpensive).

■ WHAT ARE PLUG-INS?

Plug-ins are small programs that run from within a major application (like Adobe Photoshop) and are used to add a narrowly specialized function. Because of the prominence of Photoshop, most digital imaging plug-ins are written in a Photoshop-compatible format. You don't have to use Photoshop, though; many other imaging applications (including Photoshop Elements) accept Photoshop-compatible plug-ins.

■ WHAT DO THEY DO?

Plug-ins can do all sorts of things: help you correct exposure; reduce grain in your images; correct for lens distortion; simulate traditional on-camera photo filters; add artistic effects; simulate wind, rain, and snow . . . the list goes on! Probably the most popular plug-ins are used to add creative special effects and

---

WHERE TO FIND PLUG-INS

Type "Photoshop plug-ins" into any Internet search engine and you'll probably get more hits than you can surf through. The following are some of the top plug-ins manufacturers:

Adobe
www.adobe.com
Alien Skin Software
www.alienskin.com
Applied Science Fiction
www.asf.com
Auto FX Software
www.autofx.com
Corel
www.corel.com
Extensis
www.extensis.com

Flaming Pear Software
www.flamingpear.com
Human Software
www.humansoftware.com
theimagingfactory
www.theimagingfactory.com
LizardTech
www.lizardtech.com
nik Multimedia
www.nikmultimedia.com
The Plugin Site
www.thepluginsite.com

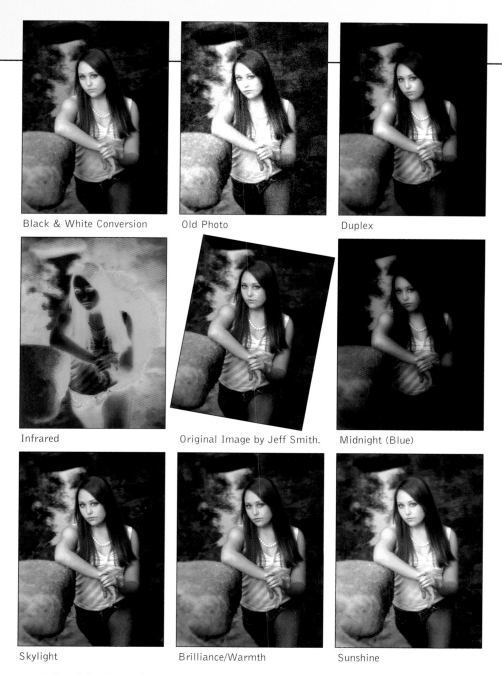

Black & White Conversion

Old Photo

Duplex

Infrared

Original Image by Jeff Smith.

Midnight (Blue)

Skylight

Brilliance/Warmth

Sunshine

specialized borders. Above is a series of images created with plug-ins from nik Multimedia. Designed for photographers, the Color Efex Pro! package features over fifty plug-ins that create effects ranging from subtle to extreme. See www.nikmultimedia.com.

29. IMAGE ENHANCEMENTS: CROPPING

It would be impossible to include instructions for every image-editing program in one book. Therefore, the techniques described in lessons 29–33 are based on Adobe Photoshop Elements, one of the most popular programs among nonprofessional photographers. If you prefer to use another program, you'll find that the basic techniques remain the same; the names of particular tools and menu items may, however, be a bit different.

The Crop tool is used to remove extraneous areas from the edges of a photo. This can improve the look of images you didn't have time to frame carefully or ones that you just didn't compose as well as you might have liked.

To crop an image, choose the Crop tool from the Tool bar. Click and drag over the area of your image that you want to keep, then release your mouse button. You don't have to be incredibly precise. At each corner of the crop indicator (the dotted line) you will see small boxes; you can click and drag

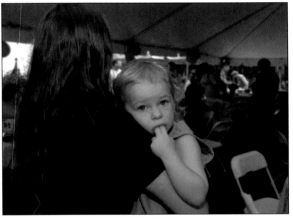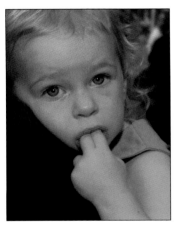

Cropping is a great way to highlight the best part an image.

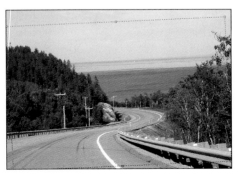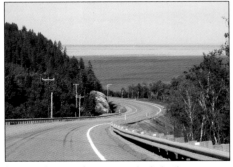

Cropping is a quick way to straighten out a crooked image, but you lose some pixels in the process.

CROPPING AND RESOLUTION

Cropping reduces the total number of pixels in an image. If you are scanning an image and plan to crop it, you may therefore wish to scan your image at a higher resolution or enlargement to compensate for this reduction. If you are working with an image from a digital camera, the total number of pixels in your image is fixed, so you'll need to determine the final resolution and image size you need and not crop the image to a smaller size than that.

these to reshape or reposition the box. (As you get near the edges of the photo, the handles tend to "stick." To prevent this, click on the handle you want to drag, then press and hold the Control key while moving the handle.) When the cropped area looks right, hit Enter.

■ STRAIGHTENING IMAGES

The Crop tool can also be used to straighten crooked images. Simply click and drag over the image with the Crop tool, then position your mouse over one of the corner handles until the cursor icon turns into a bent arrow. Once you see this, click and rotate the crop indicator as needed. Doing this may cause the edges of the crop area to go outside the edges of the image. If this happens, simply click on and drag each box to reposition them inside the frame.

■ CROP TOOL OPTIONS

In the Options bar at the top of the screen you can set the final size of the cropped image. This is helpful if, for instance, you specifically want to create a 4"x6" print. Simply enter the desired height, width, and resolution needed before cropping, then click and drag over the image to select just the area you want. The Crop tool will automatically constrain itself to the desired size.

Also in the Options bar is a setting for the crop-shield color and opacity. This shield obscures the area you are cropping out, giving you a better idea of what the photo will look like with these areas removed. Leaving it set to black will usually be fine, but you can change the color by clicking on the rectangle to the right of the words Shield Color. You can also adjust the opacity to allow the cropped-out area to be partially visible. To turn off the shield, uncheck the box to the left of Shield Color.

30. IMAGE ENHANCEMENTS: EXPOSURE

With the automatic image-correction functions in Elements, it's amazingly simple to create dramatic improvements in images that aren't quite perfectly exposed or where the colors didn't come out quite right.

That's the good news. The bad news is that Elements is, after all, a piece of software—it's not equipped with human vision. To compensate for this shortcoming when making its automatic corrections, it is forced to assume what the image is supposed to look like. For example, the software makes assumptions about the overall lightness and darkness that an image should have and about how the colors in the image should be balanced. If your images match the assumptions (and many photos actually do—they didn't pull these assumptions out of midair, after all), you can get good results—maybe even great ones—from the auto functions. When your photos don't match these assumptions, however, the results achieved with the auto functions can be downright scary.

Enhance	
Quick Fix...	
Auto Levels	⇧⌘L
Auto Contrast	⌥⇧⌘L
Auto Color Correction	⇧⌘B
Adjust Lighting	▶
Adjust Color	▶
Adjust Brightness/Contrast	▶

Go to the Enhance pull-down menu to access the auto correction features.

That said, it only takes a couple of seconds to figure out if these methods will give you the results you want, so it's almost always worth giving them a try. Just be prepared to hit Edit>Undo if you aren't happy with the results.

■ AUTO CONTRAST

The Auto Contrast command, as the name implies, adjusts the contrast of your image—and only the contrast. It will not help any color problems that might

---

FOR BETTER CONTROL . . .

You can adjust color and contrast using the tools found under Enhance>Adjust Color, Enhance>Adjust Lighting, and Enhance>Adjust Brightness/Contrast. Most of these tools can be figured out with a little trial and error. The Levels tool, however, is a bit more complex—but it's also the best tool for making really fine adjustments. For instruction on this, consult the Help files in Elements or an Elements manual (I would, of course, recommend my own book *The Beginner's Guide to Adobe® Photoshop® Elements®* [Amherst Media, 2004]).

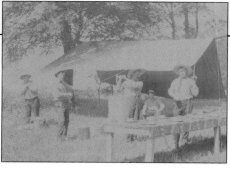
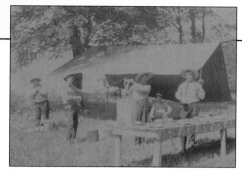
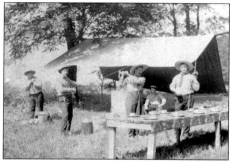
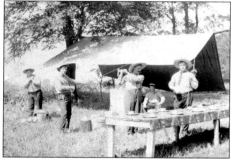

The original photo (top left) lacked contrast and had a yellow color cast. The Auto Contrast (top right) helped the contrast but not the color. The Auto Levels (bottom left) improved both the color and contrast, taking the image to a sepia tone that is probably close to what it originally looked like. The Auto Color Correction (bottom right) fixed the contrast and eliminated the color cast, rendering the photo in pure black & white tones.

be present in your photograph. If the contrast in the image you are working with seems a little flat or dull but the color looks okay, this is one strategy you could try.

■ AUTO LEVELS

Auto Levels performs a correction that is similar to Auto Contrast, except that it also affects the color of your image. Theoretically, this should remove any overall color cast—but if your image doesn't have an overall color cast, it might actually add one. Still, this is worth a try for images that need a little more contrast and have an obvious color cast you want to remove.

■ AUTO COLOR CORRECTION

This is the most sophisticated of the three automatic functions—and it works remarkably well on a lot of images. While it sometimes introduces color problems, in many images it will be all you need to get the color and contrast to a point that is quite acceptable.

31. IMAGE ENHANCEMENTS: BLEMISHES

Professional image retouching can make a portrait subject look like a million bucks. Now the same tools pros use are at your fingertips, so you never have to live with blemishes and other little problems—even in your snapshots!

◘ CLONE STAMP TOOL

The Clone Stamp tool works just like a rubber stamp, but the "ink" for the stamp is data from one good area of your image that you "stamp" over a problem area. Using this tool definitely takes some practice, but once you master it, you'll probably find you use it on just about every image.

To begin, choose the Clone Stamp tool from the Tool bar. Then, set the brush size in the Options bar at the top of the screen (the size will depend on the area available to sample from and the area you want to cover).

Move your mouse over the area that you want to clone, then hold down the Opt/Alt key and click. Next, move your mouse over the area where you want the cloned data to appear and click (or click and drag). As with the other

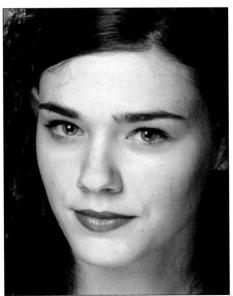 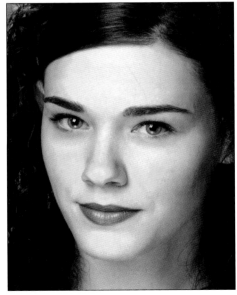

The Clone Stamp tool is perfect for removing small blemishes (left) and creating a more flawless look (right). You can even use it to remove stray hairs and shape the eyebrows! Photo by Jeff Smith.

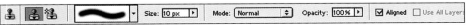

The Clone Stamp tool Options bar.

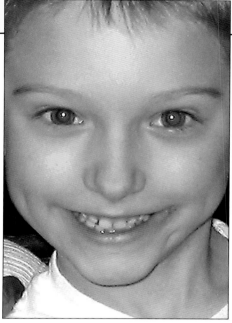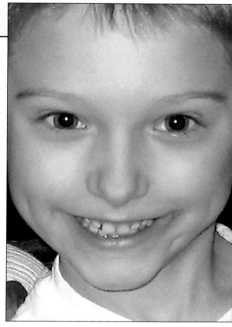

The Red Eye Brush can be used to remove red-eye (above left) and create a much more pleasing appearance (above right). The Red Eye Brush Options bar appears below.

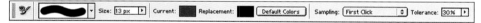

painting tools, you can also adjust the opacity of the Clone Stamp tool in the Options bar. Use the Zoom tool (magnifying glass) to enlarge your view for precise work.

■ RED EYE BRUSH

Red-eye is just a fact of the anatomy of our eyes, but that doesn't mean we have to live with it in our images. Elements makes it easy to remove the problem and create a much more pleasing look. For this correction, it will be very helpful to zoom in tightly on the eyes you want to correct.

To use the Red Eye Brush, choose it from the Tool bar, then select the brush settings you want. Click on Default Colors to reset the Current color to red and the Replacement Color to black. Then, make sure the Sampling is set to First Click. Position your mouse over a red area of the eye and click (or click and drag) to replace the red with a dull gray.

If the red isn't all replaced, try setting the Tolerance slider higher (the default 30-percent setting will work for almost every image, though).

32. IMAGE ENHANCEMENTS: SHARPENING

Sharpening and blurring are everyday operations with digital images. You can use these techniques to remedy flaws or to enhance the appearance of your subject.

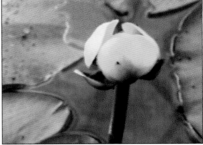

The original image was scanned from a print and needed some sharpening.

■ SHARPENING

If your image looks pretty much okay to the naked eye, but a little fuzziness is apparent when you really get critical, sharpening may do the trick. Almost every scan of an image also requires at least a little sharpening to make it look as crisp as the original.

To sharpen an image, go to Filter> Sharpen and select the tool you want to use. As noted below, some filters run automatically, while others require you to adjust their settings.

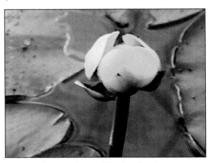

Using the Unsharp Mask, the image was slightly sharpened.

The Sharpen filter automatically applies itself to every pixel in the image or selection. It works by enhancing the contrast between adjoining pixels, creating the appearance of sharper focus. The Sharpen More filter does the same thing, but with more intensity.

The Sharpen Edges filter seeks out the edges of objects and enhances those areas to create the illusion of increased sharpness. Elements identifies edges by looking for differences in color and contrast between adjacent pixels.

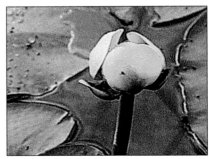

Sharpening must be done in moderation. Oversharpened photos look grainy and have unattractive light halos around dark areas, and dark halos around light ones.

Unsharp Mask is the most powerful sharpening filter in Elements. To begin, go to Filter>Sharpen>Unsharp Mask. This will bring up a dialog box in which you can adjust the Amount (how much sharpening occurs), the Radius (how far from each pixel the effect is applied), and the Threshold (how similar in value the pixels must be to be sharpened). To start, try setting the Amount to 150 percent, the Radius to 2 pixels, and the Threshold to 10 levels. Watch the preview and fine-tune these settings until you like the results.

If you're not sure you've sharpened an image correctly, go to Edit>Undo and compare the new version to the original. If the sharpened version was better, you can return to it by going to Edit>Redo.

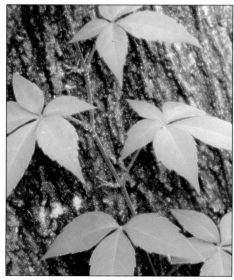

The Unsharp Mask dialog box.

■ SOFTENING

To soften an image, duplicate the background layer and apply the Gaussian Blur filter (Filter>Blur>Gaussian Blur) at a low setting (3 to 5 pixels). Then, set the blending mode of the duplicated layer to Lighten (at the top of the Layers palette). The Gaussian Blur filter and the Blur tool (used just like the Sharpening tool, as was described above) are also very useful for improving images by making distracting elements much less noticeable.

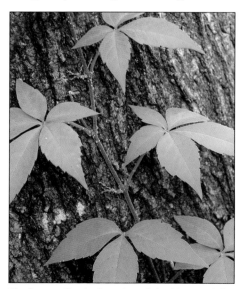

To give a softer look to the original image (left), the background layer was duplicated, blurred, and set to lighten (right).

33. IMAGE ENHANCEMENTS: COMPOSITING

The ability to composite images (using parts from two or more images to create one final image) was one of the first big advantages of digital imaging. Before digital, swapping heads in a portrait or changing a stormy sky to a sunny one was very time consuming and required the creative skills of a master darkroom technician. Today, the job is much easier. Producing totally realistic results when compositing an image still takes practice, of course. The example here is an extremely simple one, but it gives you an idea of what's involved.

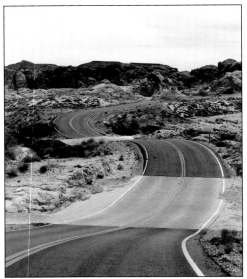

■ A BORING SKY

In the image to the left (top), the sky lacks texture and detail. There's not much you can do about that when taking the picture. To fix the problem, the image was opened in Adobe Elements.

■ SELECTING THE AREA

The first step is to select the sky area—the area we want to replace. Because the area was all pretty much the same color, the Magic Wand tool was perfect for making this selection. In the Options bar at the top of the screen, the Tolerance

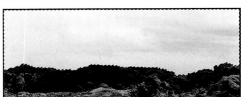

The original sky (top) was uninspiring. Selecting it (bottom) was the first step to changing it.

(how similar in value the pixels must be in order to be selected) was set to 30. The Contiguous box was also checked, ensuring that only colors in the sky area (not similar tones that happened to occur throughout the image) would be selected. Then, the sky was clicked on to select it.

■ CHOOSING A REPLACEMENT

Bald, ugly skies are a common problem. Therefore, you might want to keep a file of images with nice skies. It doesn't matter what's in the rest of the photo;

you'll only be using the sky. In this case, the sky in the whale photo (right) seemed like a good choice.

■ SELECT THE SKY

Once you've found a sky you like, use the Marquee tool to select it. Copy the selected area (Edit>Copy). Move back to your original image with the selection still active and go to Edit> Paste Into. Your new sky will appear in the selected area. If it's not positioned quite right, use the Move tool to click and drag it into place. You'll get the best results with this technique if both images are about the same size and resolution.

■ BLENDING

When the horizon line is sharp, as it is here, that's it—you're all done. With other images, however, you may need to blend the new sky into its new home. This can usually be done by care-

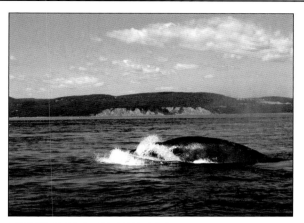

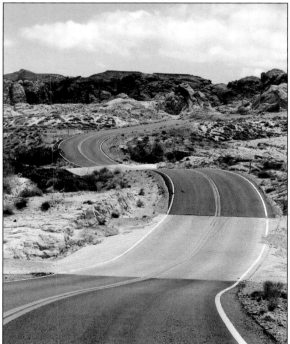

The sky from the whale image (top) was copied and pasted into the original photograph to create the image seen above.

fully using the Clone Stamp tool to remove any telltale edges around the perimeter of the selected area. This is basically the same technique as the one used to cover blemishes (see pages 66–67).

34. OUTPUT: HOME PRINTING

Purchasing a printer for your digital images can take a bit of research—there are lots of models on the market and lots of factors to consider.

■ COST

First, you'll need to consider cost—but don't look at just the cost of the printer itself. It's extremely important to check the prices, longevity, and availability of the ink cartridges. Believe it or not, these can quickly exceed the cost of the printer itself!

■ HOW WILL YOU USE IT?

You'll also want to consider how you plan to use the printer. Will you be printing photos only, or do you also need to print word-processing documents and other office materials? Photo printers provide the best results for digital images, but they can be slow (and rather expensive per page) for printing other documents.

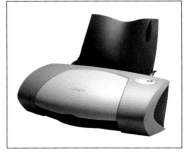

Inkjet printers are a popular choice for printing photos at home.

■ PRINT QUALITY

Print quality is also an important consideration—but don't rely strictly on resolution ratings. For example, an inkjet printer with a 1400dpi resolution actually won't produce as good a print as a dye-sublimation printer with a 300dpi resolution. Why? As you'll read below, it has to do with the way each type of printer applies color to a page.

■ INKJET VS. DYE SUBLIMATION

When purchasing a home printer, most people will be choosing from two basic types: inkjet and dye sublimation.

Inkjet printers squirt fine droplets of liquid ink onto the surface of the paper. These models tend to be inexpensive and, for most images, do a good job of producing photorealistic prints.

With inkjet printers, consider carefully the number of inks used to print images and how the ink tanks are divided up. The general rule of thumb is that the more colors of ink you have, the better your prints will look. The minimum number you will find is four (black, cyan, magenta, and yellow), but many models feature two additional colors (a light cyan and a light magenta) that enhance color reproduction. It's also advisable to purchase a model that allows you to replace each ink color individually as they run out—this will save you money in the long run.

Keep in mind that inkjet prints don't offer the same archival qualities as traditional photographs—they will fade over time (many in as little as a year or two). They can also be damaged very easily by any moisture.

Dye-sublimation printers are more expensive to purchase and to operate than inkjets, but they produce prints that look and feel much more like traditional photographs.

Dye-sublimation printers use solid inks on transfer rolls or ribbons. Rather than squirting drops of liquid ink, the solid ink is rapidly heated until it becomes a gas (a process knows as sublimation, hence the name). This allows the colors to diffuse onto the surface of the paper and provides better blending for more continuous tones. As a result of this process, the prints look smoother and have sharper detail than inkjet prints.

In addition, prints produced by dye-sublimation printers are more resistant to fading, so they last longer.

OTHER PRINTING-RELATED CONCERNS

For print longevity, your best bet is professional printing. If you must print your own images, though, look for a printer that permits the use of archival inks and papers. These are more expensive, but they offer the best chance for creating a long-lived print. Of course, inkjet technology simply hasn't been around all that long, so how even "archival" prints will hold up under non-laboratory conditions remains to be seen. Keeping prints cool, dry, and out of direct sunlight will also improve longevity.

If high volume is an issue—say, you publish an illustrated monthly newsletter for the five hundred brave folks in your skydiving club—a color laser printer (right) offers nice print quality for both text and images. These printers provide rapid printing and low per-page costs.

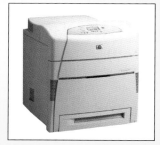

35. OUTPUT: INKJET MEDIA

Because of their low cost and good print quality, inkjet printers are the choice of most consumers for home printing. Accordingly, manufacturers have begun producing a variety of materials that put your printer to good use.

■ PAPERS

Inkjet printers employ liquid inks, and you may find that it tends to soak in and reduce the vibrancy of colors; therefore, special glossy photo-quality papers are available for use with these printers. These greatly improve the look of your images and produce prints that feel more like photos. For projects that include both photos and text, graphic arts papers offer a smooth surface that prevents excessive ink absorption, but with a matte finish that makes text easy to read. For letters, announcements, and more, you can save yourself some ink by using papers with preprinted borders and backgrounds. Thousands of designs are available.

■ LABELS AND STICKERS

Of course you can print address labels and such—but did you know you can also use your printer to produce window clings and even bumper stickers? These can be sealed using a product called Jet Coat to prevent water damage.

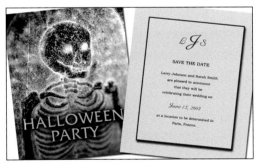

Using your image-editing software, your word processor, or even specialized greeting-card software, it's easy to print cards for any occasion.

■ CARDS

Pre-sized, perforated, and scored business cards, postcards, greeting cards, and more are available at any office superstore—and even at many larger department stores. Craft and other specialty stores also carry high-end, elegant invitation kits for formal occasions (like weddings) so you can completely tailor your invitation to your event.

■ ARTISTIC MEDIA

Textured watercolor papers are available to give your images a "painterly" feel—you can even purchase sheets of inkjet canvas to print out your masterworks. Additional artistic papers include metallics, vellum, and velour. For more kid-friendly art projects, try inkjet shrink sheets—the digital version of Shrinky-Dinks. Glow-in-the-dark paper is also available for any number of interesting projects, as are inkjet temporary tattoos! Finally, inkjet printing also lets you create embossed images. Traditionally, embossed images were made by rais-

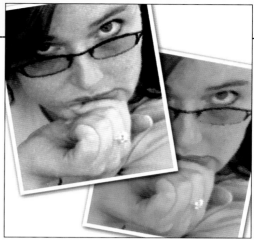

Prints made on canvas and watercolor paper have a soft, artistic feel.

ing the surface of the paper using a shaped template and embossing tool. With an inkjet print, you simply sprinkle embossing powder on the still-wet print, then apply heat to melt the powder into a raised design.

■ FABRIC

Many digital photographers are familiar with printable t-shirt transfers that can be ironed onto any cotton fabric. These are lots of fun and very easy to use—just remember to use your image-editing software to reverse your image from left to right before printing (then, when you flip the iron-on over onto the T-shirt, the photo will come out the right way).

Believe it or not, though, you can actually print directly onto fabric as well. All you need are some inkjet printer fabric sheets, available at most fabric and craft stores. These are treated with an ink fixative that protects your printed images from being spoiled by getting wet and helps them stand up to washings. Simply trim any loose threads, then load one sheet at a time into your inkjet printer. Once printed, you simply peel the paper backing off and use the fabric as you wish—in a quilt, as a patch, etc. Many people also finish their fabric prints with a UV-protectant coating to reduce the potential for fading due to harsh light exposure.

■ DIRECTIONS

It goes without saying, but it's important to follow the directions on all these projects—both to ensure success and to have a safe creative experience.

36. OUTPUT: LAB PRINTING

For some images, an inkjet print is just fine—especially when you just want a cute new photo to stick on the refrigerator or on the front of a greeting card. Other images, however, require more permanence and the best-possible quality. You wouldn't, for instance, want the prints in your daughter's baby album to fade before she's even out of nursery school.

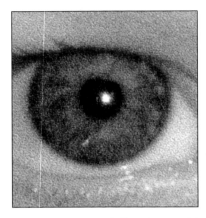

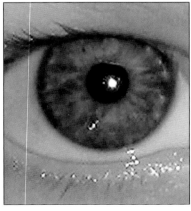

Inkjet prints are made up of tiny dots. This is revealed when the image is enlarged. Compare the detail in the eyelashes in the inkjet print (top) and the lab print (bottom).

■ REAL PHOTOS

Many people don't know they can get prints made from their digital files on the same paper and equipment used to make prints of their film images. So why make the trip to the lab? There are a lot of reasons.

True photographic prints are created using photosensitive paper and a series of chemicals rather than inks sprayed onto regular paper. This means that the tones in the image are continuous, not made up of tiny dots. As a result, the prints look crisp and details tend to be much more sharp.

The papers and processes used to create true photographic prints are time tested. Your images will still be around for your kids and grandkids to enjoy—especially if you keep them dry and out of direct sunlight.

Let's face it, printing your own images is time consuming—especially if you want multiple sets in multiple sizes. The prints from a lab can be made in a variety of standard sizes and can be produced with matte or shiny surfaces, depending on your personal preferences.

Best of all, in addition to lasting longer and looking better, lab prints are cheaper than prints you make yourself. Most photo labs will make a 4"x6" print from your digital file for somewhere in the neighborhood of twenty to thirty cents.

■ WHERE TO PRINT

Many drugstores, grocery stores, and department-store mini-labs now have the ability to make true photographic prints from your digital files—you just take in your memory card or CD and select the images and print sizes you want. In about an hour, your prints will be waiting for you.

The same goes for your neighborhood camera shop—take in your disc and pick out your prints. You can expect to pay slightly more here, but you'll also have the benefit of a more experienced staff that knows how to bring the best out of every image.

Online printing is very easy and affordable—and you'll usually receive your prints in about a week. Online labs have some other nice features as well. Most allow you to set up albums of images to share with friends. This is great for images of big events like reunions—you just upload your photos and e-mail a link to the site to your family or classmates. They can then order whatever prints they want directly from the site, so you don't have to worry about who wanted what and how to get it to them. Many online labs also offer an assortment of borders and text you can add to your images, as well as an assortment of fun photo products that can be ordered right along with your prints. Some even have professional image retouchers available who can tackle tricky jobs you aren't prepared to do yourself. Best of all, most online photo labs will let you try out their service for free. Typically, they provide about ten free prints when you set up a new account. You'll need to spend a couple of dollars on shipping, but you'll get a good sense for how the site works and the quality of their images.

ONLINE PHOTO LABS

www.agfa.com	www.hpphoto.com	www.smugmug.com
www.aol.com	www.mpix.com	www.snapfish.com
www.bonusprint.com	www.ophoto.com	www.togophoto.com
www.clarkcolor.com	www.photoaccess.com	www.walmart.com
www.clubphoto.com	www.photoworks.com	www.winkflash.com
www.dotphoto.com	www.printroom.com	www.xpphoto.com
www.ezprints.com	www.ritzcamera.com	www.yahoo.com
www.fujifilm.net	www.shutterfly.com	www.yorkphoto.com

37. OUTPUT: OTHER PHOTO PRODUCTS

Online labs, neighborhood mini-labs, and even many copy shops now offer photo products that go way beyond prints. These make great gifts and are another way to showcase and share your best images.

■ TYPES OF PRODUCTS

Calendars. Many different styles are available, but your most basic choice will be between models that have twelve photos (one for each month) and one photo (with twelve monthly tear-off sheets underneath it).

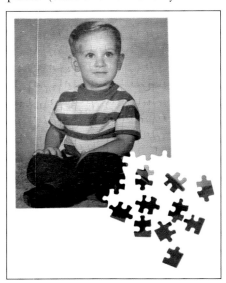

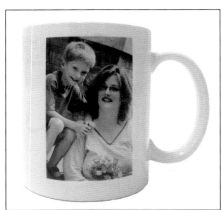

Photo puzzles and mugs are quick to make and fun to share.

Games and Toys. Photographic jigsaw puzzles (often nicely packaged in a box that also bears your photo) are widely available. You can also purchase playing cards with your photograph printed on the back, a Rubick's cube with a different photo on each side, or even a teddy bear wearing a t-shirt with your photo on it.

Stationery. In this category there is a wide variety of choices—note cards, notepads, notebooks, postcards, stickers, envelopes, labels, Post-it® cubes, and more.

Domestic Items. Photo mugs have been available in mall kiosks for years, but how about a frosted-glass photo beer stein, or a stainless-steel photo travel mug (bound to make your daily commute a little nicer)? Other good gifts for around the house include mouse pads, fridge magnets, place mats, coasters, trivets, night-lights, and more.

Textiles. Photo t-shirts (in a variety of styles and colors for everyone from infants to adults) are available at many online photo labs. Many labs also offer photos on canvas tote bags and chef's aprons. Some let you use tiny versions of a favorite image in a mosaic pattern that is applied to ties and scarves. You can also find photo pillows, purses, makeup bags, and quilts.

Jewelry. You can actually have a photograph either etched or enameled onto either silver or gold. For women, there are lockets, pendants, bracelets, earrings, and more. For guys, look for key chains and tie pins.

Food. Some web sites offer photo chocolate bars, cookies, lollipops, and more. Most larger grocery stores now can also print your photograph on a cake to celebrate a special occasion.

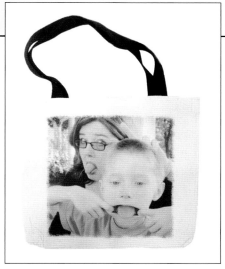

Tote bags can be personalized with a fun family photo.

■ SPECIAL EFFECTS

Many sites will also allow you to add special looks to your images before purchasing products. These may include the addition of text, fancy borders or seasonal frames, or artistic effects like an overall watercolor texture. If these interest you, look for a site that provides a good range of options.

RESOLUTION

The following are the minimum resolution requirements for creating prints at most sites. For photo gifts, the size of the product (and the photo on it) will determine the needed resolution—so the photo needed to create a locket will be smaller than the one needed to create a mouse pad or t-shirt, for example. Check with the company you plan to order from before purchasing.

wallet print . . . . . . .419x279 pixels	11"x14" poster . . . .1600x1143 pixels
4"x6" print . . . . . . .640x480 pixels	16"x20" poster . . . .1920x1536 pixels
5"x7" print . . . . . .1050x750 pixels	20"x30" poster . . . .2272x1500 pixels
8"x10" print . . . .1280x1024 pixels	

38. OUTPUT: ON THE INTERNET

When preparing images for the Internet (on a web site, as an e-mail attachment, etc.), the desire for quality must be balanced with the need to minimize file sizes. After all, it won't matter how great the photo is if the people you want to see it get tired of waiting for the file to load and give up. The following strategies can be employed to whatever degree you see fit.

■ SAVING FOR THE INTERNET

Color Mode. Online, most images are used in the RGB color mode (see page 13). Using the Indexed Color mode, however, allows you to limit the total palette of colors used in your image, reducing the file size while retaining visual quality. At most, the Indexed Color mode allows you to use 256 colors, but you can also use fewer than 256 colors, reducing the file size and image quality in the process. The trade-off between load time and image rendition is a subjective one. If your image-editing software supports this color mode, you can experiment with the settings and your resulting file sizes; you may find a very happy medium between great color rendition and load time—especially in situations where extreme color fidelity is not required.

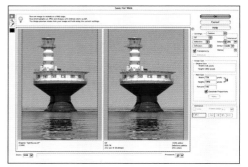

The Save for Web tool in Adobe Photoshop Elements helps you optimize your images to maximize their quality and minimize their load time.

File Format. Saving your file in the JPEG format can reduce the file size and the load time, generally without severely impacting the look of the image. For this reason, most online photo labs require your images to be in the JPEG format before they will allow you to upload your files.

Optimize for the Web. Some image-editing programs offer special tools for optimizing your images for online viewing. In Abode Photoshop Elements, this is called the Save for Web feature (File>Save for Web). With this tool, you can instantly preview your optimized image side by side with the original image as you adjust a number of size-reducing settings. You can also check the approximate load time for your image. The settings you choose will depend on your own preferences, but you may be surprised at how much you can reduce your file sizes while maintaining very acceptable quality.

■ SHARING YOUR IMAGES

E-Mail. Probably the most common use for photos online is as e-mail attachments (little packages of data that are sent with a letter). These are then downloaded and opened by the recipient. This is a great way to share single photos with lots of people, since one e-mail message can be addressed to a number of recipients.

Web Page. More and more people are setting up their own web pages—a fun way to share your photos! Many Internet service providers give subscribers special tools for setting up a personal web site, so consult yours if you are interested in this option. You can also set up a free account on some web sites and receive a little space to set up your site. Most free sites offer limited storage space, but it's enough for a simple page with a few of your favorite images.

Photo Albums. Many web sites allow you to set up a free digital photo album. These are easier to use than setting up your own web site, but they don't give you quite as many options in terms of how your photos are displayed and labeled. However, many sites do offer the convenience of placing print orders right from your album. Online albums work well for sharing multiple images—say, all the photos from your birthday party or family vacation.

More and more people are setting up their own web pages—a fun way to share your photos!

■ EXPANDING YOUR SKILLS

The Internet is actually a great place to refine your skills. In addition to visiting other photographers' sites and seeing how they handle their subjects, you can visit sites by both professionals and amateurs with photo tips, tutorials, and step-by-step techniques. If you're really interested in learning, you can join a photo discussion group or community. These allow you to get feedback on your images and may even challenge the members with specific photo assignments—a great chance to compare your images of a subject with the way other photographers present it. For more formal learning, photo courses are also available for a fee. Normally, these give you access to weekly lessons and feedback on your images from a professional photographer.

39. WORKFLOW

With digital, the image-creation process doesn't end when you click the shutter—it's just getting started! The term "workflow" is commonly used to describe everything that happens to a digital image file in the time between when it is shot and when it is output and/or archived.

■ SECURITY

When you shoot digital images, your files are the equivalent of your negatives with film photography. If you lose them, damage them, or accidentally delete them, it's all over—you'll need to reshoot the image if you want or need to use it again. The best way to ensure that this won't happen is to develop a routine that you will use every time you come home with new images.

■ AN INDIVIDUAL WORKFLOW

The specific details of the process that will work for you will depend on how much you shoot, how much time you have to spend archiving your images, and how you want to use your images. The following steps will, however, be included in just about every workflow.

> When you shoot digital images, your files are the equivalent of your negatives.

Upload Your Images. The first step will be to upload your images to your computer. You can do this from your camera or using a card reader—whatever works for you.

Burn a CD. Once the images are uploaded, you should immediately burn a CD (or DVD) of all of the original, unaltered image files. For the most reliable backups, choose a brand-name CD rather than the cheapest pack on the office-supply store's shelf. Five, ten, or fifteen years out, there really is a difference between the longevity of the brands.

Label the CD Clearly. Label this disc clearly, noting the date and adding a few words about the photos. Over the years, you may acquire hundreds of these CDs, so be specific. You may know what you mean now when you write "Wedding" but ten years from now you'll probably appreciate the extra effort it took to write "Chris and Noël's Wedding (October 10, 2004)."

Test the CD. After burning this CD, test it out on your computer to ensure that it reads properly and that the image files open.

Store the CD Safely. This CD should be stored in a secure place where it won't be exposed to moisture, excessive handling, or great heat. If you have room, you can store your CDs in plastic jewel cases. You can also store them in paper sleeves and place them in a sturdy box or filing cabinet. CD wallets and binders can

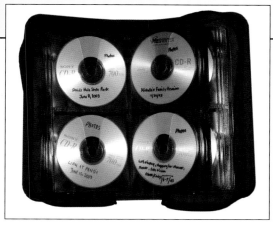

Binders used to store music CDs also work very well for archiving discs of digital images.

also be very useful—especially because they make it easy to keep your image CDs in sequence (which can make it easier to track down a particular one).

Sort Your Images. The next step is to return to the images on your computer and look through them. You may want to make subfolders to separate out your favorites or to differentiate the subjects (say, if you visited the Washington Monument and Smithsonian Institute on your trip to Washington, D.C.).

Edit Your Images. Once you've decided which images you want to print or share with friends, or use on your web site, you can make any needed changes to perfect these files. Making this process a secure one is covered in the next lesson.

Burn a Second CD. Editing and retouching your images requires a significant investment in time. Therefore, it's a good idea to make a second backup at this point. Consider including both your retouched and original files on this disc and storing it in a different location—maybe at work or at a friend's house. As horrible as it is to think about, in the event of a fire, flood, or other disaster, you'll be happy you made the effort.

Output. The next phase of your workflow will depend on how you want to use your images. Refer to lessons 34–38 for more on this.

Reformat Your Memory Card. Once you've completed this entire process, you can safely reformat your memory card and reuse it for your next pictures. Depending on how much space you have on your computer's hard drive, you can hang on to all the images there or toss out any files you won't be needing in the future.

40. CONTACT SHEETS

With film, photographers laid their strips of negatives across photo paper and exposed them in the darkroom to create a single sheet that contained tiny versions of each image on the film. Because these prints were made with the negative in contact with the paper, they were called "contact sheets." The same idea lives on with digital—and contact sheets are still just as useful.

■ MAKING CONTACT SHEETS

Most digital-imaging programs will allow you to automatically make a contact sheet from all of the images located in one folder. In Adobe Photoshop Elements, you just go to File>Print Layouts>Contact Sheet. This will bring up the dialog box seen below. In it, you can select the folder that holds the image files you want to appear on your contact sheet. Next, choose the size of your contact sheet (if you'll be printing on 8½"x11" paper, leaving it at the default setting of 8"x10" will be fine). Set the resolution as you like, depending on whether you want to print the contact sheets or just view them on your monitor. Then, select how many rows and columns of images will appear on each page. The

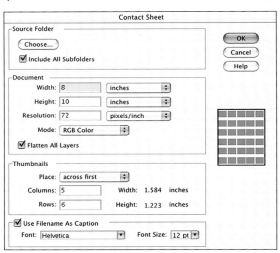

The Contact Sheet dialog box.

more rows and columns you choose, the smaller each thumbnail image will be. Finally, choose the "Use File Name as Caption" option. As shown in the finished contact sheet (facing page), doing this will make it much easier to find the particular image you want.

■ CONTACT SHEETS FOR QUICK REFERENCE

Contact sheets can be stored with backup image CDs for quick reference or used to contrast different versions of an image, as suggested on the facing page.

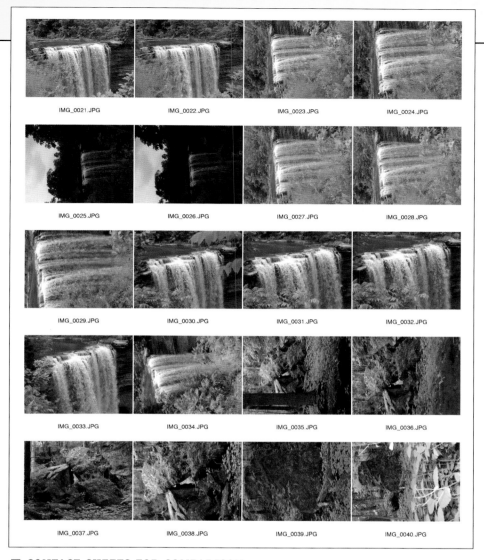

IMG_0021.JPG   IMG_0022.JPG   IMG_0023.JPG   IMG_0024.JPG

IMG_0025.JPG   IMG_0026.JPG   IMG_0027.JPG   IMG_0028.JPG

IMG_0029.JPG   IMG_0030.JPG   IMG_0031.JPG   IMG_0032.JPG

IMG_0033.JPG   IMG_0034.JPG   IMG_0035.JPG   IMG_0036.JPG

IMG_0037.JPG   IMG_0038.JPG   IMG_0039.JPG   IMG_0040.JPG

■ CONTACT SHEETS FOR COMPARISON

Sometimes it can be tricky to decide if you prefer version A of an image to version B. If this happens, try printing a contact sheet of the two (or more) images you want to consider. Seeing the different versions side by side can make the choice more obvious.

You can also show these sheets to people and get some feedback. Often, we become so familiar with our own images that we see what we want to see in them; a fresh set of eyes can help bring us back to reality and promote better decision-making.

85

CONCLUSION

Digital imaging has revolutionized photography. Taking great pictures of your family, friends, pets, vacations—whatever your heart desires—is now easier than ever. You can shoot limitless photos and only pay to print the ones you love. You'll never leave a birthday party or family reunion wondering if your pictures will come out—thanks to the LCD screen, you'll know exactly what you got. And if not every shot is perfect, you can usually fix it in a few seconds—then e-mail it to all your friends and family. While the learning curve is a little steep, the rewards are great—and having finished reading this book, you're well on your way! Good luck and enjoy!

ABOUT THE AUTHOR

Michelle Perkins is a writer, designer, and photographer specializing in landscape and architectural images. She has written for *PC Photo* and is a regular contributor to *Rangefinder*, amagazine for professional photographers. She is the author of numerous books including *The Beginner's Guide to Adobe® Photoshop®*, *The Beginner's Guide to Adobe® Photoshop® Elements®*, and *The Practical Guide to Digital Imaging*, all from Amherst Media.

GLOSSARY

Aperture—The opening in the lens that light passes through to make an image. If it's wide, the scene will fall out of focus as objects recede from the point on which you are focused. If it's narrow, more of the scene will be in sharp focus.

Aperture Priority Mode—This mode is usually denoted by an "Av" on the exposure dial or menu. It allows you to select the aperture while the camera sets the shutter speed.

Archival Quality—The ability of a medium to resist deterioration over time. The term is often used to describe prints that resist fading and color changes.

Artistic Effects Mode—Often indicated by a palette and brush, this mode allows you to select from color options that may include shooting in black & white or sepia tones as well as vivid color (enhanced color saturation and contrast) or neutral color (subdued color saturation and contrast).

Auto Mode—On digital cameras, a setting where the camera makes all the decisions about exposure, focus, flash, white balance, etc. This mode is good for fast shooting under changing conditions and for inexperienced camera users.

Bit Depth—Indicates how well a scanner can differentiate between colors.

Burst Rate—The number of images a camera can shoot in rapid sequence before it needs to pause and process the files. High burst rates are good for photographers who like to shoot fast-action subjects like sports.

Byte—A single unit of digital information.

Card Reader—A device used to transfer data from memory cards without the need to connect your digital camera to your computer.

CCD—The type of image-sensor chip found in most digital cameras. These produce excellent image quality but are more expensive to manufacture than CMOS chips. *See* CMOS.

CD Burner—A device that allows you to write data onto CD-Rs.

CMOS—A type of image-sensor chip found in some digital cameras—particularly digital SLRs. This chip has some advantages when producing really high resolution images and is less expensive to produce than CCD chips. *See* CCD.

CompactFlash—A type of memory card used by many digital cameras.

Compositing—Combining parts of two or more photographs (or other types of images) to create one final image.

Composition—The art of carefully designing an image and consciously deciding how to frame a scene or subject. *See also* Rule of Thirds.

Compression—A system of arranging image data more efficiently (or removing data deemed extraneous) in order to reduce the file size.

Contrast—The difference between the lightest and darkest tones that appear in the image.

Cropping—Removing extraneous areas from the edges of a photograph.

DVD Burner—A device that allows you to write data onto DVD-Rs and/or DVD-RWs.

Dye-Sublimation Printer—A type of printer in which dry colorants are rapidly heated to a gas state then transferred to and solidified onto paper.

File Format—The "language" in which the digital image is written. Tells an application how it should handle the data in the file to display it correctly.

File Size—The amount of memory required to store and/or process an image. The larger the file size, the more space required to store it and the more time required to perform operations on it.

Filter, Digital—Used within image-editing software to apply a specialized effect to an image.

Filter, Photographic—Transparent material that attaches to the lens of a camera and allows you to adjust the light entering the camera in creative ways.

FireWire—A type of high-speed data transfer between peripheral devices (like card readers and external hard drives) and a computer.

Flash Memory—Memory cards that are solid state, meaning there are no moving parts (electronics rather than mechanics do the work).

Focal Length, 35mm Equivalent—Lenses function at a different *effective* focal length depending on the size of the image-sensor chip being used. Because the size of the image-sensor chips in digital cameras vary widely, manufacturers base their listings of focal length on the size of a classic 35mm film frame.

Focusing, Close—A setting on many digital cameras that allows you to bring your lens to within a few inches of your subject and still get a well-focused shot.

Gamut—The extent or range of colors that can be produced or displayed by a particular device (such as a monitor or printer).

Gigabyte (or GB)—A unit of data measurement equal to a billion bytes. The storage capacity of computer hard drives and digital camera microdrives is often described using this unit of measurement.

Grayscale—A color mode that consists of only one channel—black. You can create a quick black & white photo from a color original by switching to this mode.

Hard Drive—The memory used to store files and computer applications that aren't in use.

Highlights—The lightest areas in your image.

Highlights, "Blown Out"—Highlight areas that are so overexposed that they lack any detail.

Histogram—A graphic representation of the tones in an image. This can be viewed from within most image-editing software and on the LCD screens of many cameras when reviewing images.

Image Modes—On digital cameras, preset shooting options designed to produce good results with a particular kind of subject (landscapes, portraits, etc.).

Image Sensor—With digital, the part of the camera that captures the image. Its unique qualities determine the resolution of the images captured on it.

Image Stitching—*See* Panoramic Images.

Indexed Color—Allows you to limit the total number of colors in your image, reducing the file size while retaining visual quality.

Inkjet Printer—A type of printer in which tiny drops of ink are squirted onto paper (or a different type of media).

Interpolation—The process of inserting extra pixels into a digital image to increase its size or resolution.

ISO Setting—On a digital camera, how sensitive to light the image sensor is set to be. Higher ISO settings allow you to work more easily in low light but produce more noise, which can reduce the image quality.

JPEG—A common file format for digital images. The JPEG format employs lossy compression to reduce the memory required to store images. This can also result in a loss of visual quality.

Kilobyte (or KB)—A unit of data measurement equal to one thousand bytes. The memory required to store a low-resolution digital image file is often described using this term.

Landscape Mode—A shooting mode in which the camera will select the smallest practical aperture in order to keep as much as possible of the scene in focus.

LCD Screen—A screen on the back of a digital camera that is used to access menus, compose images, and review photographs.

Lens, Fixed—Common on low-end point-and-shoot models and minicams, this type of lens offers only one view of a scene or subject.

Lens, Interchangeable—A lens that can be removed and switched.

Lens, Zoom—A lens that lets you choose between several views of a scene. You can zoom in (use a telephoto setting) to get a closer view or zoom out (use a wide-angle setting) to see a broader view.

Light Meter—An instrument built into digital cameras that measures the light reflected off a subject and recommends an appropriate exposure setting.

Macro Setting—*See* Focusing, Close.

Manual Mode—On digital cameras, a setting where the photographer makes all the decisions about exposure, focus, flash, white balance, etc.

Megabyte (or MB)—A unit of data measurement equal to one million bytes. The storage capacity of digital camera memory cards and the file size of images are often described with this unit of measurement.

Megapixel—A measurement of the image size a particular digital camera's image sensor can capture.

Memory Card Reader—*See* Card Reader.

Memory Cards—Devices used to store digital images after they are captured by the camera's sensor.

Metering—Evaluating the amount of light in a scene to determine the correct exposure.

Microdrives—A type of memory card that is actually a miniature hard drive (just like in your computer).

Midtones—All of the tones in an image that are neither pure white nor pure black.

Movie Mode—Most point-and-shoot models let you take short, low-resolution movies. They can also, however, eat up lots of space on your memory card, so be sure to buy a large media card if you want to shoot these regularly.

Native File Format—A file format that is associated specifically with one application program (such as a particular type of image-editing software). It is usually optimized for this program.

NiCd (Nickel Cadmium)—A type of rechargeable battery. *See also* NiMH.

Night Portrait Mode—An image mode that allows you to balance a dark background with a flash-lit foreground subject.

NiMH (Nickel Metal Hydride)—A type of rechargeable battery that offers longer life and more rapid recharging than a NiCd battery. *See also* NiCd.

Noise—A grainy appearance in digital images that occurs when using high ISO settings or may be added intentionally using image-editing software to create a desired look.

Panoramic Images—Long, narrow photographs that often show as much as a 360-degree view of a scene. Many digital cameras now offer a mode that helps you shoot a sequence of images that you can later combine into a single panoramic shot using software. This is often referred to as "image stitching."

Peripheral Device—An external device that is connected to a computer. This could include printers, scanners, external hard drives, digital camera card readers, etc.

Pixel—Short for "picture element," a pixel is the smallest discrete part of a digital image.

Platform, Computer—The operating system a computer runs on and is designed around—for example, Windows or Macintosh. While users of one system or the other may have personal loyalties to their platform of choice, it really doesn't matter that much which one you decide to use.

Plug-ins—Plug-ins are small programs that run from within a major application like Adobe Photoshop or Adobe Photoshop Elements. Because of the prominence of Photoshop, most plug-ins are written in a Photoshop-compatible format. You don't have to use Photoshop, though; many other imaging applications (including Photoshop Elements) accept Photoshop-compatible plug-ins.

Portrait Mode—A shooting mode in which the camera will select the widest practical aperture in order to allow the area behind your subject to go quickly out of focus, making it visually less distracting.

Program Mode—The program mode (usually indicated by a "P") allows you to control some settings (like white balance, ISO, etc.) but not as many as the fully manual mode.

PSD—A file format used by Abode Photoshop Elements to save images without flattening any layers that are included.

RAM—This is the memory your software and images are loaded into when you open them. If you have too little, things will get really slow. Check your software to determine its minimum requirements—and add more RAM if you need to.

Red-Eye Reduction—Red-eye occurs when the lens and light source (usually an on-camera flash) are directly in line with the subject's eyes. There are two ways to combat this effect. (1) Most cameras now include a red-eye reduction setting. When this setting is used, an initial burst of light closes down the pupil, preventing the second burst of light from reflecting off the retina and back into the camera (which is what makes the center of the eye look red). (2) If red-eye still occurs, you can fix it easily in your image-editing software.

Refresh Rate—On monitors, high refresh rates help reduce screen flicker, which in turn reduces eye strain and (in some people) headaches.

Resolution, Image—How close together the pixels (dots) in an image are. Expressed as dpi (dots per inch).

Resolution, Monitor—For monitors, resolution is expressed in terms of pixels and lines—for example, a 640x480 monitor displays 480 lines of 640 pixels. Virtually all monitors can support 640x480 pixel resolution (also called "VGA" resolution). In order to display more information on the screen, most models also offer at least one "Super VGA" setting—often 800x600 or 1600x1280 pixels. Some monitors offer settings at even higher resolutions.

Resolution, Optical—On a scanner, how much data can be recorded by the image sensor itself. Other, larger figures may be listed, but these values are obtained by using software to enlarge the file; this reduces the quality of the scanned image.

Retouching—Using image-editing software to reduce or correct problems in an image that were unnoticed or impossible to correct at the time the image was taken.

RGB—The color mode in which scanners, digital cameras, and monitors—devices that receive or transmit light—all capture or display color.

Rotate—To turn a selected area of image data (or the entire image) around a fixed point.

Rule of Thirds—A guideline for composition designed to help photographers place subjects in the frame to maximum advantage. By this rule, a tic-tac-toe grid of lines is mentally placed over the whole frame. The intersections of these imaginary lines are generally the best places to position the center of interest in a photograph.

Save—To preserve an image for future use (including further editing, viewing, and/or use in another application).

Scale—To change the size of a selected area of image data.

Scanner, Flatbed—Device used to digitize photographic prints and other flat, reflective surfaces.

Scanner, Transparency—Device used to digitize photographic negatives and slides.

Shadows—The darkest areas in your image.

Sharpen—To increase the apparent focus of an image (or area of an image) to enhance the clear reproduction of image detail.

Shutter Lag—A delay between when you push the shutter button on a digital camera and when the photo is actually taken.

Shutter Priority Mode—In this mode (commonly indicated by "Tv"), you select the shutter speed and the camera selects the best aperture setting to match the brightness of the scene. Choose a short shutter speed to freeze moving subjects, or a long one to blur them.

Shutter Speed—How long the camera's shutter remains open to make an exposure. When you (or your camera) choose a long shutter speed, subjects in motion will be blurred in your image; when you choose a short shutter speed, subjects in motion with be frozen in your image.

Sports Mode—When you use this mode (sometimes also called a burst or action mode), your camera will keep taking images for as long as you hold down the shutter button. This will continue until either your memory card runs out of storage space or your camera runs out of processing memory and has to pause before shooting the next image.

TIFF—A common file format for digital images. The TIF format employs lossless compression to reduce the memory required to store images. This preserves the visual quality of the image.

Timer—Like most point-and-shoot film cameras, your digital model will probably have a timer that allows you to set the camera and then duck into the shot.

USB—A type of high-speed data transfer between peripheral devices (like card readers and external hard drives) and a computer.

Viewfinder—With digital cameras, a window (like on a traditional film camera) that can be used to compose images with the camera held up to your eye.

White-Balance Settings—Settings designed to balance the colors in a scene for accuracy under just about any kind of light—sunlight, fluorescent light, tungsten light, etc.

Workflow—An individualized procedure followed when uploading, backing up, editing, and archiving images. This is designed to safely and efficiently process digital files.

Zoom, Digital—On a digital camera, this is image enlargement that is provided by software rather than the lens. This reduces the image quality and should usually be avoided. *See also* Lens, Zoom *and* Zoom, Ooptical.

Zoom, Optical—On a digital camera, this is image enlargement that is provided by the mechanical qualities of the lens. This produces sharp images. *See also* Lens, Zoom *and* Zoom, Digital.

INDEX

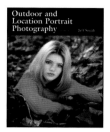

OUTDOOR AND LOCATION
PORTRAIT PHOTOGRAPHY, 2nd Ed.

Jeff Smith

With its ever-changing light conditions, outdoor portrait photography can be challenging—but it can also be incredibly beautiful. Learn to work with natural light, select locations, and make all of your subjects look their very best. This book is packed with illustrations and step-by-step discussions to help you achieve professional results! $29.95 list, 8½x11, 128p, 80 color photos, index, order no. 1632.

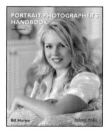

PORTRAIT PHOTOGRAPHER'S HANDBOOK,
2nd Ed.

Bill Hurter

Bill Hurter, editor of *Rangefinder* magazine, presents a step-by-step guide to professional-quality portraiture. The reader-friendly text easily leads you through all phases of portrait photography, while images from the top professionals in the industry provide ample inspiration. This book will be an asset to experienced photographers and beginners alike. $29.95 list, 8½x11, 128p, 175 color photos, order no. 1708.

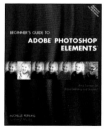

BEGINNER'S GUIDE TO
ADOBE® PHOTOSHOP® ELEMENTS®

Michelle Perkins

This easy-to-follow book is the perfect introduction to one of the most popular image-editing programs on the market. Short, two-page lessons make it quick and easy to improve virtually every aspect of your images. You'll learn to: correct color and exposure; add beautiful artistic effects; remove common distractions like red-eye and blemishes; combine images for creative effects; and much more. $29.95 list, 8½x11, 128p, 300 color images, index, order no. 1790.

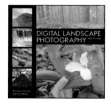

DIGITAL LANDSCAPE PHOTOGRAPHY
STEP BY STEP

Michelle Perkins

Learn how to capture the drama and majesty of nature. Using a digital camera makes it fun to learn landscape photography—and provides instant results so you can instantly learn from each successful shot you take. Short, easy lessons ensure rapid learning! $17.95 list, 9x9, 112p, 120 color images, index, order no. 1800.

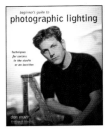

BEGINNER'S GUIDE TO
PHOTOGRAPHIC LIGHTING
Don Marr

Learn how to create high-impact photographs of any subject (portraits, still lifes, architectural images, and more) with Marr's simple techniques. From edgy and dynamic to subdued and natural, this book will show you how to get the myriad effects you're after—and you won't need a lot of complicated equipment to create professional-looking results! $29.95 list, 8½x11, 128p, 150 color photos, index, order no. 1785.

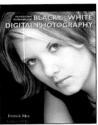

PROFESSIONAL TECHNIQUES FOR
BLACK & WHITE DIGITAL PHOTOGRAPHY
Patrick Rice

Black & white photography is an enduring favorite among photographers—and digital imaging now makes it easier than ever to create this classic look. From shooting techniques to refining your images in the new digital darkroom, this book is packed with step-by-step techniques (including tips for black & white digital infrared photography) that will help you achieve dazzling results! $29.95 list, 8½x11, 128p, 100 color photos, index, order no. 1798.

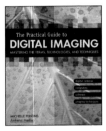

THE PRACTICAL GUIDE TO DIGITAL IMAGING
Michelle Perkins

This book takes the mystery (and intimidation!) out of digital imaging. Short, simple lessons make it easy to master all the terms and techniques. Includes: making smart choices when selecting a digital camera; techniques for shooting digital photographs; step-by-step instructions for refining your images; and creative ideas for outputting your digital photos. Techniques are also included for digitizing film images, refining (or restoring) them, and making great prints. $29.95 list, 8½x11, 128p, 150 color images, index, order no. 1799.